LIVES AND
LOVES IN CARS

LIVES AND LOVES IN CARS

Alex Dellasandro:

With assistance of Master Mechanic Joe Aile

AUTHORS NOTE: Any resemblance in this account to persons
living or dead is coincidental. The cars and their performances are
real.   ADA 2004

This book was printed in the United States of America.

To order additional copies of this book, contact:
Xlibris Corporation
1-888-795-4274
www.Xlibris.com
Orders@Xlibris.com
26062

CONTENTS

Foreword 9

A 1933 Plymouth Coupe 11

A Put Together 1940 Plymouth 19

A 1939 Buick Sedan 27

A 1941 Plymouth Sedan 35

A 1949 Dodge Wayfarer 41

A 1957 Ford Fairlane 47

A 1953 Chevrolet Convertible In Spain 53

A Karmann Ghia 61

A Fiat 124 Sport Sedan 69

A 1972 Buick Convertible 77

A 1979 Lancia Sedan 85

A 1982 Mercedes Turbodeisel 95

Infiniti Q45 1990 103

Infiniti Q45 2002 111

To all auto mechanics everywhere.

FOREWORD

That Americans love, even lust after automobiles, is a foregone conclusion and nothing really new. Steel and chrome, lately fiberglass, aluminum and plastic, have allures that trigger the genes and hormones of most men and many women. This attraction is more than biology. It is part of a great American tradition. Most of us recall, in voluptuous detail, the shapes, colors, and styles of cars now long gone. We can still feel their road handling, shift characteristics and cornering ability in our bones and sinews.

This is true romance. The landscapes and adventures of youth and maturity can be seen in glimpses of bygone cars, in old movies, photographs, and during nationwide popular antique car rallies. Special girls who rode in those cars reappear including memories of romantic things kids tended to do when parked. As an inevitable result, soon after, wives and children rode in later models. Either way, love, courtship and family became involved.

This romance comprises much more than misplaced nostalgia. Each vehicle symbolized a particular period of life and the peculiar history and tensions of its times. Each became a talisman of things to come. Some became milestones toward freedom. Each offered an ever-present means of escape to distant places, new adventures, and new opportunities, and each became part of the landscape of childhood, youth and adult lives. Many decry automobiles as energy wasteful, polluting machines. Their skeletal hulks and old tires litter the landscape. Yet, we still love them as much as ever, and as personally as we loved friends and companions and family who rode in each of them.

A 1933 PLYMOUTH COUPE

Anthony DeAngelo bought a 1933 Plymouth coupe in Yonkers, New York in 1947 just as he turned fifteen. At that time, beginner's driver's licenses were available in Westchester County at fourteen. World War II ended in 1945, and few new cars were on the road. Chrysler Corporation built about 21,000 of these popular rumble seat coupes. They had real running boards and were priced new at $535, a considerable amount of money in 1933.

He had saved money from odd jobs, and had a talented friend, Andrew Wegmann, a classmate from his Yonkers public school. He paid $120 in cash for the coupe rebuilt over years by Andrew in his garage. The young mechanic, who later went on to engineering school, had completed the project before he could get a driver's license. At the time of this transaction, a soft, colorful Indian summer, Andrew and Anthony were beginning juniors at Bronxville High School.

Anthony's mother offered concerns, but no serious objections, though they worried about how to pay for repairs. They were not well off: Anthony's father had died just five years previously. Luckily, Andrew had done a superb job of rebuilding. Repairs were not required, save for replacing a fuel pump. The car was always driven low on gas. One dollar's worth, about three gallons, was a standard refill purchase for a high school boy, and he could not afford insurance. He had one minor accident, a fender bender that he acknowledged as his fault, though the other driver struck the left rear of the coupe as it pulled slowly away from a curb near school. An old man, driving a Mercury, angrily claimed that Anthony had not signaled properly, so he paid thirty-five dollars in cash to repair minor damage to the right front fender of the Mercury. The solid steel of the Plymouth remained unblemished.

For the time he owned the Plymouth, until beginning college, no mechanical mishaps troubled the little gray coupe. Although he had been taught not to "lug" the engine, it easily negotiated the hills of Yonkers, often in third gear. The low gear ratios were highly favorable for this purpose. The car weighed 2,500 pounds, and its special option, high compression, six-cylinder engine delivered 76 HP at 3600 rpm. The car stick shift was on the floor, typical of cars at that time. The steering wheel had a "suicide" knob attached that you could steer with one hand, leaving the other arm free for shifting gears. Its main purpose was to facilitate placing an arm around a girlfriend. A crank orifice resided below its vertical grill. This was needed only once to turn over the engine after a long absence while he served in an infantry regiment at National Guard Camp. Each morning during junior and senior years, he drove north from the old neighborhood to High School. In the afternoons, the coupe carried Anthony cross-town to swimming practice at the Yonkers YMCA and to work in the Physics Research laboratory at a Textile Company in the Nepperhan Valley. The company gave him a parking place inside the wire gate. Here, in the fall of 1949, he happened to be standing by the car just as Harry Truman spoke during his campaign against a stodgy, overconfident Governor Thomas Dewey. Later, he learned about Truman's humble beginnings and his success as an artillery Captain during War One. Even at that time he could see, as Truman spoke in confident, hopeful tones to the crowd in that mean factory yard, that the modest man from Missouri knew what it meant to work hard for a living.

The coupe became Anthony's passport to new worlds, work, athletic endeavor, and, not the least romance, if prospects of lustful adventure, constantly in the minds of adolescent boys, could be called that. The knob on the steering wheel aided these efforts, though, at that time, he had no concept of the seriousness of those female consorts who sat, unbelted close to him on the bench seat. Extraneous girls and other boys rode in the rumble seat, ignoring inclement weather to snuggle down for the pleasure of the ride

Within two days of getting the pink slip, he attempted to go parking to "make out". High school classmates, with the abundant wisdom of the uninitiated, suggested Sprain Lake Reservoir, a wooded area next to a picturesque lake in Westchester County. So with Edie O'Hara, a sophomore on board, he drove the coupe into the woods on the edge of the lake on a fine early autumn night. Second base happened quickly; as he, in amazement, felt her perky breasts with remarkably erect nipples. It was cool, so they each closed their window, which quickly fogged up. Abruptly, blinding flashlights, shouting, and figures seen dimly through the windshield startled them. A deep voice with an Irish accent ordered them out of the car. They struggled, each out of different doors, adjusting their clothing in a rude glare of light. "Arrah, Mother of God, do ye see who this is?" said one burly cop to his partner. He learned that his date was a police captain's daughter. They were sent home, but not until the officers told them that the only reason that they would not be reported, so that Anthony would lose his beginner's license for driving after dark, was that, surely, her father would kill them both. Irish cops were stern but fair, and a whole generation of New York kids, having caused not a few troubles for them while growing up, remains indebted to their humanity. The police rendered on the spot discipline, which might include a slap or two, without turning young miscreants to a justice system that, likely, would have done more harm than good.

Later, Edie invited Tony to an all night New Year's party in the Bronx at an Irish relative's house. They were to be chaperoned, but all the adults were drunk by midnight. Edie must have had in mind the completion of the act they had started at last fall at Sprain Lake. By then, having met and learned of her father's reputation, Anthony had gotten true religion, a true fear of God and tried nothing. By dawn's light, Edie was furious: Anthony learned a bitter lesson of 'Woman Scorned'. They drove back to Yonkers in painful silence. She never spoke to him again.

During football season, seven or eight kids crammed into and upon the car, some hanging off the running boards, all on their way to cheer for Bronxville High. The springs held and the car retained plenty of power. They played a perilous game called "Spider". One pair of eyes sat up to steer and two kids got down on the floorboards to run the clutch and accelerator; a fourth manned the gearshift. The eye person, steering, gave verbal commands. They became quite expert at this foolish trick, and found it hilarious when the car stopped, four people alighted where only one had been seen at the wheel.

The coupe became the exclusive domain of one girlfriend, a quiet dark eyed girl of Russian or Polish descent called "Ank" for Anyaka. She lived in the Nodine Hill Parish above the carpet factory and belonged to a group of girls his friends called "Hill Skwac". These girls had the reputation of being less inhibited than Bronxville High School girls, and Ank proved to be a passionate and generous lover. They met, far from the waspy confines of the Bronxville crowd, at a Polish Community Center dance on the west side of town. Anthony thought her as fine as some exotic, silent queen as they drove together in the coupe up and down the hills of Yonkers. Evenings ended parked unobtrusively on a back street on Nodine Hill not far from her home. Ank must have had a trace of Mongolian heritage: long straight black hair, high cheekbones and almond eyes. She wore long skirts that modestly reached to just above her ankles, went to Yonkers

High School, a blue-collar milieu much different than that of Bronxville High, and tolerated his clumsy lovemaking with infinite patience. They managed to make love on the cramped bench seat, she sitting on his lap on the passenger side, avoiding the annoyance of the stick shift in the middle of the cab. They sat facing each other while the ledge at the back of the coupe gave her leverage for her arms so that she could control motion and penetration as she desired.

Only gradually did he come to understand that Ank, loving and fine as she was, needed to play for keeps. They hung out together for almost two years and were happy. Anthony skipped his senior prom, though one of the Bronxville girls had asked him to be her escort. He wanted to show off his exotic Nodine Hill girlfriend. Ank told him that she felt uncomfortable about going to a prom with "all the sharpies in the Bronxville Crowd." She let him know that she was destined for the altar not college. They parted gently, almost imperceptibly: Anyaka married a factory hand in late August after high school graduation. That fall, Anthony put the coupe in the garage in Yonkers, went downtown to Columbia College, and saw Ank no more.

During freshman year at Columbia, Arthur O'Neill came back on leave from basic training in the army. Arthur, a tough kid in the old neighborhood, wanted to learn to drive, and Anthony felt he owed him, having beaten him in a boxing match just before Arthur left to join the army. They went out in the Plymouth together. Arthur could not get the knack of handling the clutch, which he rode continually all the while racing the engine. Finally, with great noise and foul smoke, the clutch burned out after a few blocks of Arthur's stop and go driving. They pushed the car for a mile and into

Anthony's garage. Arthur felt badly, but on $21 per month army pay he did not have money to pay for repairs. The vacuum clutches on the 1933 Plymouths were complicated, featuring a free wheeling option and also an installation option that allowed the transmission to operate without depressing the clutch pedal. Anthony did not need a car at college.

With a sad heart, he called a man from a junkyard who arrived with a tow truck. The old man started the engine, listened to it carefully and looked thoughtfully at the Plymouth for a long time, inspecting its fine gray finish, stately vertical grill and shiny chrome bumpers. The man then turned to ask Anthony if he wanted the clutch replaced. When he heard the cost of repairing the unique vacuum clutch, Anthony could barely speak. He did not have that kind of money. The man scratched the stubble on his chin, shook his head, handed Anthony thirty-five dollars and towed his beloved coupe away.

Fifty years later during the Hot August Nights auction in Reno, Nevada, Anthony saw an exact rebuilt replica of his gray 1933 Plymouth rumble seat coupe. Recalling Edie and Ank and those wonderful days and nights, tears came to his eyes. Thinking practically, perhaps too practically, he resisted the impulse to buy the car on the spot. Perhaps, he should have yielded to his heart. A 1933 rumble seat Plymouth coupe could have been a great hit in the Hot August Nights Parade in Sparks, Nevada.

A PUT TOGETHER 1940 PLYMOUTH

In the spring of 1952, Anthony's best childhood friend, Danny, one of eleven children of the Sullivan family who lived in a large sprawling house on Villa Avenue in Yonkers, sold him, for ten dollars, a ramshackle 1940 black Plymouth sedan. It had a stick shift on the steering column and two wired on fenders. The headlights were taped and glued in place; one windshield wiper worked on the driver's side. The tires were fair, the car started reliably, but its chassis rattled endlessly. Apart from an erratic voltage regulator, detected when the ammeter registered failure to charge, the car ran well. From time to time, whenever the ammeter registered in the negative zone, Anthony opened the hood to manually reset the voltage regulator contacts. Eventually, though he was not at all adept at car repair, a local mechanic helped him install a $14 junkyard voltage regulator.

Junior year at Columbia College had just ended and next fall he was headed toward Medical School in New York City. This car, put together from spare parts by Danny, proved to be a lifesaver. He had summer work as a lifeguard at Tibbets Brook Park, an awkward commute from his Yonkers home, making this transportation important. Danny had developed severe childhood diabetes at age fourteen. In retrospect, it became clear that Danny had decided not to live. The Plymouth was a gift to Anthony. During freshman year of medical school, each day he drove the to the elevated at Gun Hill Road for the ride down town to medical school. Apart from its voltage regulator, the car cost not another cent save for gas and regular oil changes. The engine burned no oil whatsoever, a symptom, as Anthony later learned, of serious, expensive trouble that, in his economic circumstances, would have presaged ruin. A breakdown on the East or West Side Drive in New York could be a major financial disaster. Fortunately, the put together Plymouth never failed, yet worries and unease nagged him when driving the old car in New York City

Early on a summer's evening, Anthony walked up to Sullivan's house to pick up the pink slip, which Danny had left with his father, Patrick, a portly red-faced man, who was recovering from a recent heart attack. The car was parked in tall grass in the backyard. The pater familias had a visitor, a

Mr. Danny Shannon, and they were sharing, morosely, a single bottle of beer. Sullivan's eldest daughter, Susan, had hidden his beloved now forbidden whiskey. After telling Anthony stories about his father, according to them a great poker player and all around good guy, the two Irishmen suggested he go down the hill to Sherwood Park to buy a fifth of Seagrams. He knew he was being conned when they gave him money, including part of the ten dollars in bills he originally had handed over for the car, along with spare change that Gannon dug out of his pocket. When Anthony returned with the whiskey, they invited him to stay. Around a table in the heart of the kitchen, the three of them sat drinking, talking, and laughing in their seductive Irish way. They quickly finished the fifth of whiskey.

As time passed and the contents of the bottle dwindled, the atmosphere became magically warm and friendly. Old man Sullivan told jokes and delved into Anthony's life. As he was involved with an Irish girl at the time, Sullivan and Gannon solemnly advised to him to make a good confession and marry her. He was sent out for another bottle of whiskey, staggering down the hill to Sherwood Park and back up the Sullivan house. They were all drunk when Susan came home. With a tongue lashing worthy of *Angela's Ashes,* she chased both of them out of the house. Anthony lurched down Villa Avenue to his home, leaving the put together Plymouth in the yard. He crawled up stairs; somehow his bedroom appeared out of reach. He collapsed in the bathroom at the top of the stairs, and slept in the bathtub. Luckily, he awoke before his mother, then caught the bus to Yonkers Avenue, and suffering intensely, walked a mile to Tibbets Pool. Though sober, his sweat still reeked of alcohol while he sat on the lifeguard chair in the morning sun. The chief lifeguard, Fagan, mercifully sent him to sleep for the rest of the morning in their break room.

The next night, when Anthony returned for the car, Susan refused to let him in. Danny was away somewhere, but had connected the battery and turned the engine over. Anthony drove the car out of the back yard, over a curb and two blocks down to the house on the corner of Kimball and Villa Avenues. That year, while Anthony was in medical school, Danny died. He amiably drank himself to death while paying little attention to his severe diabetes. Before he died, they both drove, from time to time, in the Plymouth to jazz bars and clubs in Harlem and Mt Vernon where Danny appeared as a regular and beloved fixture. They shared free drinks given "on the house" to white kids in these jazz clubs, but DeAngelo never had the chance to say goodbye to his childhood companion. On two occasions in later life, when Anthony had been critically ill, he dreamt of seeing and laughing once again with his friend with the blue eyes and easy smile.

The sedan ran without fail the winter of that first year. He drove it around Manhattan, figuring if it broke down, the plates could be removed and the car left along with other derelicts. He parked it in an old lot behind Bellevue by the East River. Its door locks did not work, but no one ever touched it. On a Saturday night in early fall, Anthony and a classmate, who lived in a duplex on Madison Avenue, went to a Yorktown dance hall in on East Eighty Sixth Street where he asked a lively English girl named Margaret Hoxley to dance. She spoke with a charming accent and seemed out of place in the dance hall crowd, mostly girls from outlying boroughs, telephone operators or office workers. She wore a blue chiffon flowered dress that reached well below her knees: both her garment and demeanor made her seem out of place. She told him she was a medical student from Dublin, who had come, under circumstances that she declined to reveal, to live in Queens with her aunt and uncle. They were attracted to one another immediately and stayed together for every dance. Anthony was impressed to discover that, in response to his questions that she really had studied and knew Cunningham's Anatomy in impressive detail.

After she made a phone call, they left their companions. His Madison Avenue friend, though wealthy, inevitably always forgot to carry cash. Anthony settled their bar bill, then he and Maggie, as she preferred to be called, spent the rest of night together in the put-together sedan parked, with a view of the East River and Brooklyn Bridge, on a quiet side street. She was passionate and surprisingly expert with her hands and mouth. He reached between her legs, pulling wet underwear aside: even this aspect of her clothing seemed foreign. These must be "knickers" he thought. With his left hand he reached for his billfold to extract a prophylactic, so long compressed in one of its compartments that it had left a circular impression on the wallet's leather. They were in the front seat and he then rolled it on his third erection of the night. She looked intently at him, hiked up her curiously long dress, undid old-fashioned garters, mounted and slowly lowered herself on to him, staring into his eyes the whole time. He felt a curious resistance, then a sudden giving away. She settled onto him slowly, wincing and seeming have some pain, but never the less letting him know that she liked what they were doing. Later, in the light, he saw blood on his shorts and groin. She volunteered that she had fooled around with her old boyfriend but that this was her first time to go all the way. Then she wanted to attend six o'clock mass, and after this, they drove to a modest home in Queens. He asked why an English girl would be going to mass. She told him that she was really Irish. He let this mystery pass but now grasped the reason for their immediate attraction. Mystical Irish kids and passionate Italians in the old neighborhood had tendencies to combine like elements in heat generating chemical reactions. Dr. Volino, an old neighborhood doctor, on doing Anthony's required physical examination for medical school had asked, in a hoarse croaking voice, if he had a girlfriend,

"Yes."

"She Irish?"

"Yes sir!"

"Don't marry her; they fight like hell", he growled.

The next weekend, Anthony arranged to meet Maggie in the Stage Door Café on 44th Street near Times Square close to the office where she worked at what she told him was a trivial job. He watched her from a corner booth as she entered the darkened tavern. She looked like a frightened little girl, in an odd foreign appearing coat that seemed oversized for her frame. She was no beauty; rather, she had a gamine face, framed by straight nondescript brown hair. She appeared touchingly vulnerable and needy. Her face lit up with joy as he stood to greet her. His heart reached out to her. He now needed the old Plymouth even more, as they spent more and more time together in Cue Gardens. They fell into a routine of drinking scotch whiskey on Friday and Saturday nights and attending mass on Sunday mornings.

Her family made no objections about their staying out all night, but the put together Plymouth drew sarcastic comments from his girlfriend's family, notably from her uncle, a former Spitfire Pilot, who had survived the Battle of Britain. By spring, he knew he had to look for another car.

And so Anthony parted with his ten-dollar rickety put-together Plymouth. The same junkyard man who had bought his 1933 Plymouth Coupe came to get it. The old dealer looked at the sedan this time with disdain, commenting on its dirty windshields and the absent windshield wiper, "How d'yah steer it, by radar?" Then he towed it away free of charge. Parts for 1940 Plymouths were still in demand.

A 1939 BUICK SEDAN

This Buick, a flawless dark royal blue, remains, many decades later, a vehicle of extreme beauty and style. One owner, a Mr. Kennedy, who lived in Tarrytown, north of Yonkers, had lovingly cared for the elegant sedan. Its immaculate gray interior upholstery contrasted with a glowing simonized exterior. Anthony settled on a price of one hundred and sixty dollars. He had fallen in love with both a girl and a car, as his first year of medical school ended. Mr. Kennedy had been honest: intimating that the motor burned oil and would soon need its piston rings replaced. A straight eight-cylinder engine, clean and powerful looking, resided beneath it shiny hood. But, as he soon was to learn, the Buick's engine was already fatally flawed. Nonetheless, he was entranced: love like lightening is just as likely to strike an outhouse as a church steeple.

At the time, he believed that could not afford to replace the piston rings, though his mechanical high school friends could have accomplished the needed repair. Instead, he went with a Polish friend to an auto store in downtown Yonkers where they bought several tubes of a kind of brown goop. This stuff, touted as "A Ring Job in a Tube", was supposed to help with the piston seal. They squirted a goodly amount of the viscid paste into each cylinder and replaced the spark plugs, which, on starting the engine, immediately became fouled. After cleaning the plugs several times, the engine ran smoothly, all eight cylinders purring power. This temporary solution proved to be a false economy. On weekends, he drove the sedan back and forth from Yonkers to Long Island to see his green-eyed and increasingly demanding girlfriend. Her uncle, seeing the Buick, put aside his beer and spoke with him, appearing to now to approve of him a bit more. In mid-summer, after a long night out in Queens, an eerie comet like tail of sparks began shooting out of the exhaust pipe as he drove across the Whitestone Bridge. He stopped in the far right lane. A patrolman, witnessing the multicolored display, pulled up behind the car expressing genuine concern. Neither of them had seen anything like this before. They lifted the hood and raced the engine; the exhaust comet seemed to diminish, so with police blessing he drove back to Yonkers and continued to drive it that way all summer.

The car provided them privacy; convenient motels were then non-existent. At first, out of habit, they continued to make love in the front seat, until Maggie suggested they retreat to the roomy back seat. Here she would assume a full missionary position, and with thighs fully flexed, she planted her feet on the upholstered roof to enhance leverage. The first time she did this the old joke about "footprints on the ceiling upside down" became apparent, and out of respect for the car, she later removed her shoes to spare its fine upholstery.

Soon, oil consumption increased alarmingly. On the advice of a mechanic at a gas station on Yonkers Avenue, he increased crankcase oil viscosity from 30 to 40 weight, and finally to 50 weight, always carrying an extra quart or two for his nightly trips over the Whitestone Bridge to Long Island. Then something else happened. On accelerating and abruptly releasing the accelerator, a deep-throated grumbling could be heard from deep within the engine block. When he added 60-weight oil to the crankcase, the rumble became muted yet ominously persistent. These sounds signaled trouble with bearings, a grave and even fatal engine illness. The bluff mechanic on Yonkers Avenue told him, sadly, that rebuilding this engine would be exorbitantly expensive. An affordable engine replacement could not be found.

That fall, the mechanic's assistant in the Yonkers Avenue shop, who knew its history, fell in love with the elegant blue sedan. Anthony warned him, as did his boss, about the bad bearings, but the young man offered to buy the car for sixty dollars on the spot. Anthony took the cash and signed the pink slip, thinking that the apprentice would repair the engine. The young man, to show off, drove it around Yonkers; a week later the engine threw a rod and destroyed itself. Margaret had, at the same time, become difficult. He had brought her home to meet his mother, and some weekends, they stayed in Yonkers. She slept in a guest room upstairs, but each morning, after his mother descended the stairs, she would quietly appear at his bedside, her lips and eyes carefully made up, to fellate Anthony's inevitable morning erection. She was clever at it, and they never got caught.

Soon her troubles began to mirror those of the Buick. She told him that she was going to Canada to marry her former boy friend, who had emigrated there from England, the same older man, apparently, who had taught her the repertoire of seductive tricks. One day she seriously angered Anthony by making a play for his summer sidekick, John Fokane. After a minor quarrel with Anthony, she decided to share the back seat with his taciturn friend. Through the rear view mirror, he saw her reach for John's crotch. Johnny, always loyal, moved away from her side with a silly laugh. Anthony could see John, with sheepish eyes, also looking at him through the mirror.

This attempt to plant horns on his head was disturbing enough, but there were other times, when she and Anthony were making love, that she would suddenly blurt out that she hated him. Her erratic actions, outbursts and mood changes appeared sudden and unprovoked. She seemed intermittently insane. Anthony might have lived with mood changes, but her pass at his friend sealed her fate. This move hurt him deeply, during entire the time that he had been seeing her, he never thought of, looked at or dated another woman. It was not that she was particularly beautiful: her breasts were small and mound-like, the nipples were decorated with a few dark hairs; her ankles were a bit thick and would likely become more so with age. Her charm resided in bright green eyes, clear white skin, and ebullient good spirits when not in one of her dark moods.

On their last night together, she apologized, finally disclosing the reason she had left Dublin. She had, as a child been told that her father was dead, then learned that she was the illegitimate child of an Anglican Clergyman and an Irish mother. Her father had come to see her, and the shock of this encounter was so great that she could not bear to stay in Ireland with her mother. Anthony reassured her that this was no big deal, but then, in Dublin and to her, such a union was, indeed, serious miscegenation. They spent a passionate night in the back seat of the Buick, watching sunrise near Ildewild Airport. As da Vinci once wrote, the male organ has a mind and life of its own. That night became a double-digit affair. He said he loved her and told her none of that Dublin stuff mattered, but, inwardly, he worried about her erratic outbursts. Apart from those concerns, he told her that he was still not ready to marry. That night Maggie appeared ecstatic, her eyes glowing in reflected light. She seemed transported into a tantric trance, like a Hindu priestess acting out some sacred erotic rite. He could not believe, after a night of such intense sex, that she really planned to leave him for an old boyfriend. He fully believed that she was bluffing. Margaret caught an afternoon flight to Toronto. Anthony mourned his losses, the girl, and the Buick, as an overwhelmingly demanding second year of medical school engulfed his life.

The Buick and the young woman seemed inextricably linked. One was a mechanical trap; the other an impending biological trap. He learned that that many women, with marriage in their sights, forget romance to become dreary pragmatists. But then, he had enjoyed great times with Maggie, driving the Buick to Manhattan to dance at places like the Starlight Roof, the Inn at Central Park, and the Statler Hotel. They were treated like royalty whenever they drove up in the blue Buick. Anthony wanted matters to continue that way for a while. Margaret had different ideas.

Worry about grumbling bearings and the constant need to add engine oil kept Anthony awake on long nocturnal journeys between Queens and Yonkers. He knew that his engine might blow up and also that his girlfriend would leave, but he found himself uncharacteristically passive and powerless to act. Knowing little about engines, he was not in a position to learn; he lacked the expertise of his high school friends. He also knew little about women. His medical school classmate, Weinberg, destined to become a psychiatrist, tried to comfort him about the loss of his volatile girlfriend. The aspiring psychiatrist knew less about female psychology than Anthony did. Though well to do, in addition to chronically forgetting his wallet, his classmate had done something exceedingly offensive. One summer night, while Anthony and Maggie were making love in the Weinberg family's deserted Madison Avenue Duplex, his clumsy friend, as usual getting nowhere with his date, tried to intrude. He entered the guest bedroom in a creepy apologetic way. Anthony jumped up and offered him a black eye instead, ending what had started as an agreeable evening and a viable alternative to fucking in a car. Anthony was looking for alternatives because Maggie had told him that, in England, they could drive through the countryside to a farm or field for a picnic and find pleasant places to be undisturbed. She seemed to so long for this, that Anthony tried to recreate her bucolic fantasies, but the best he could do, at least in New York City was to take her to Long Beach. It was not possible for unmarried couples to check into decent Manhattan hotels for part of the night, and Long Beach proved unsatisfactory: love-making in the sand on a windy beach late at night proved to be less than comfortable.

After Maggie left, the embryonic psychiatrist succeeded, in his smarmy way, to make Anthony feel even worse than he did about her sudden departure. He confided the whole story to his swimming coach. When Coach Smith heard his tale, he shook his head. His advice was abrupt and proscriptive, "Forget it; you're not ready to take some one like this on now." Anthony tried to forget her, but it seemed as if he had lost part of his body. He remained ill for several weeks with nausea and vomiting, lost ten pounds but eventually recovered his composure.

Anthony regretted not having learned about engines, and would have wanted to become as familiar with their innards as he had become with human anatomy, but he had never had the time. However, mechanics, usually honest, always helped. He had gotten sound advice about the Buick from one mechanic, but felt guilty about the young apprentice who had to junk the car. The temptation to drive it was just too much for the kid. It would be five years until Anthony was able to buy a new car. Meanwhile, he again studied newspaper ads and this time went with high school classmate, Roberto Trimarco, an accomplished mechanic, to look at his next prospective purchase.

A 1941 PLYMOUTH SEDAN

Chrysler products survived long after World War II ended in 1945. Remembering Danny's gift, Anthony responded to an advertisement in the *Herald Statesman* for another Plymouth, a 1941 model, residing in a tidy suburb in Northwest Yonkers. This car, an immaculate two-toned blue and metallic gray sedan, was slightly shorter in wheelbase than the previous Plymouth. This model had "suicide doors" named for the way the rear doors opened, with the hinges toward the back of the car. The US Navy and Army requisitioned these cars early in 1941 to become the highly reliable P11 staff cars. The Army painted them olive drab, but the Navy kept their original colors: photographs can still be found of an admiral with his staff exiting the four-door sedan to a group saluting them. These cars had a six cylinder, 201.3 cubic inch L-head engine, which developed 87 horsepower at 3800 rpm. The transmission offered 3 speeds with low gear ratios and required steady clutch engagement to avoid bucking.

The Plymouth sedan had been acquired by an older couple just before the war began, and they were lucky to have had it. They were asking $195, swore that it ran well, and appeared devastated to part with their precious car. The elderly wife actually wept when Anthony took it for a test drive. As touching as their story was, the reasons for used car sales, Anthony had learned, always need careful scrutiny. Anthony drove the car twice and the second time he brought his mechanic friend, Roberto, because he heard a hint of a faint but ominous deep-throated rumble deep in the block of its six-cylinder engine. The oil pressure also appeared to be low when racing the engine after warm-up.

Roberto told him that the main bearings could be replaced with oversized ones and that the crankshaft, probably only minimally deformed or "out of round", could be reground. The two of them negotiated a price of $120 for that immaculate car and Anthony turned it over to his friend. After two weeks, quite pleased, Roberto returned the car. The engine now ran smoothly and showed oil pressures of 45 to 50 psi. Roberto did this extensive repair for about $80. Anthony drove the Plymouth all through his second and third year of medical school, but the car met an untimely violent end in the spring of 1955. During that time, the car had proved itself invaluable. Totally reliable and trouble free, it carried him to work as a lifeguard and then to a lucrative summer job that paid six dollars an hour doing construction on a bridge on the Hutchinson River Parkway. At that time, he became a dues paying member of both the International Hod Carriers and the Teamsters Unions.

The car had an annoying feature, a gas-powered heater that the elderly couple had installed. They were quite proud of it. The contraption sat on the passenger's side and when turned on ignited electrically by some arcane process, independent of the engine heat. In midwinter, it generated either too much or too little heat. The bulky gadget glowed fitfully, all the while making nasty rasping noises. In the cold weather, he did not wish to park in the car for any extended period. He never understood the operation of that anomalous heater, constantly worrying that it might blow up, a preoccupation not at all conducive to romance in a parked car.

That fall, his second year of medical school, academic and social life revolved around the reliable pristine Plymouth. He began to date a graduate student who attended his physiology class. She, and one other remarkably well-endowed young woman from White Plains, became its main passengers. Eventually the reserved graduate student, Anne, won his affection. She lived in Hackensack, New Jersey. Return journeys across the George Washington Bridge in the early morning hours now became the weekend custom. He had developed enough confidence in the car to commute to his hospital rotations for clerkships during junior year of medical school, and found himself relieved to suffer no surprises, either from the car or his new girlfriend.

He and the petite blonde graduate student dated every weekend, driving around in New Jersey along Routes 4 and 17 to nightclubs and roadhouses that featured live music with two bands for nonstop dancing. Evenings ended by eating hamburgers and drinking coffee in a shiny New Jersey diner on Route 4. One summer night while driving south on Route 17, after seeing a lurid drive-in movie, the back of the car seemed to explode. As the front seat gave way, they were thrown into the rear while the car, driven by an unknown force, accelerated to 70 miles an hour. He managed to scramble to the steering wheel first, steering wildly to avoid a bridge abutment, then pulled himself forward to reach the brake pedal. They clambered through the sprung rear doors, wondering at the destruction of the rear end. The "suicide" door feature had provided their escape route. While they were puzzling over the source of the damage, a distraught young man appeared, running towards them down the dark roadway. Crying and apologizing, he wailed that he had fallen asleep at the wheel. His out of control unlighted car had struck them from behind with such force that they were propelled out of sight. The Plymouth was totally wrecked.

Insurance offered him only $75 for his irreplaceable vehicle. But, and this was a big but, Anthony and Anne both complained of stiff necks. When a New Jersey doctor started ultrasound treatments, the insurance company settled with him for $500 and paid Anne, a similar amount. Anthony convinced her that they could stop seeing the ultrasound quack who wanted to treat them *ad infinitum*. He took her to Rye, New York for a ride on the Roller Coaster that was well tolerated by their necks. The settlement barely covered the cost of his next purchase, also a Chrysler product. That fall, Anthony and Anne were married in an Episcopal Church in Hackensack New Jersey. The destroyed Plymouth had provided a dowry.

A 1949 DODGE WAYFARER

The Dodge came from a used car dealer on Route 4 in New Jersey, and cost four hundred and fifty dollars, the bulk of the insurance settlement he had received for the rear end collision. It carried a three-month guarantee, something quite novel for Anthony. The transaction was completed in a day. Anthony needed to return to work in Yonkers and had neither time nor transport to search newspaper advertisements or to test cars. The few days he was stranded in New Jersey, Anne's parents kept them on a tight leash, never once offering him one of one the two cars they kept locked in their garage. He noticed that these were careful people who kept plastic covers on their furniture. When they finally extricated an old Mercury out of the garage so that Anne could take him to the Dodge dealer, the three of them spent fully twenty minutes in the driveway washing the windshield and all its windows.

The Wayfarer, now only five years old, was relatively new compared to the other cars he had owned. Its gearshift was on the steering column: the car had a clutch, with a hybrid transmission that operated both manually or automatically. Chrysler Motors had called this novel, though inefficient arrangement, a "gyromatic" transmission. In low gear, its automatic mode yielded a peculiar sluggish action, and engine power was such that it took 16 seconds to reach 50mph. It was hard to tell whether it was the engine or the power train yielded the mushy sliding action characterizing that car.

Anthony owned the Dodge when he and Anne married in 1955: they drove it until they bought a new car in 1957, a first for Anthony. He used the Wayfarer for summer work, commuting to Manhattan Hospital during his last year of medical school. They commuted together in the Dodge from the Bronx to Manhattan and back. They had rented an apartment on McLean Avenue near Bronx Parkway, driving to New York's East Side Drive via Bruckner Boulevard, a dismal potholed route passing through vicious south Bronx slums. Roadwork on the benighted roadway had never ended during the time they lived in New York. Someone much later published a book called *Are They Are Still Building Bruckner Boulevard?* He despised that dismal route, appropriately chosen for a disastrous encounter with a gang member in *Bonfire of the Vanities.* One night, on Bruckner Boulevard, a patrolman gave them a citation for a burned out taillight that the young couple could ill afford.

The Dodge navigated downtown Manhattan during the summer before his senior year, while Anthony worked as a detail man for Schering Corporation, calling on fancy doctor's offices on the East Side of midtown Manhattan. The company's premise was that a medical student would more easily gain access to busy practitioners. This cachet, plus kind words for the receptionist, effectively gained detail calls. Prednisone, a revolutionary powerful form of cortisone, had just been introduced. Schering also promoted an effective antihistaminic called Chlortrimeton. The Dodge's trunk was loaded with samples of these drugs that the doctors seemed to prize. Anthony's visits had to be strategically timed so that he could move the car at exactly 11 AM from one side of the street to the other, to avoid being ticketed and towed as each side of the street was cleaned on alternate days. During that long hot summer, he learned a great deal about the travails of salespeople. This was a job he was sure that he would not want do again. Much later after he developed a successful practice, detail people were welcomed in his office. However brief their interchange, Dr. De Angelo always asked that they put his name down for a "full visit". In late afternoon, when his required calls had been done, he picked up Anne at the Fifth Avenue Medical School for the East Side Drive-Bruckner Boulevard trek. The mushy, sliding performance of the Dodge seemed well suited for Manhattan's sluggish traffic.

Before beginning internship in New York, he and Anne took their first real vacation. They planned to drive the Dodge for a two-week trip to the Florida Keys for Scuba diving. They spent a good portion of their budget to purchase a regulator, a tank and two masks and pairs of flippers. They practiced diving with their new equipment in the pool where he had worked as a lifeguard. At that time, formal courses for Scuba Certification did not exist, but they became sufficiently competent after practicing in the swimming pool. With diving gear and a fully pressurized air tank stored in the trunk, they drove south on Route One on their first extended automobile trip. Anthony had never been South of New Jersey before, and, as they drove further south, found that he had difficulty understanding people at gas stations and diners. In North Carolina, a good-looking waitress brought grits with their breakfast eggs, teasing Anthony in her broad drawl, when he asked what "gri-i-its" were. She became flirtatious and, in the style of southern women, charming in her speech that seemed to hang upon on his every word. The overall effect was startlingly seductive, as compared to the negligent nasal conversational tones of New York women. His wife glared at the waitress and she broke off the conversation. He was pleased to learn about grits for breakfast, and, there and then, he began to like the South and its people.

Late one afternoon in the middle of rural Georgia disaster loomed. They first thought they imagined it: a subtle sound coming from the rear end. On entering the town of Benniston, an ominous whine from the rear end had become unmistakable. The unhealthy noise got louder and higher in pitch by the minute, signaling serious transmission trouble. They stopped at a gas station where they were directed to a garage run by a man named "Red". The couple's little vacation appeared done for. Red looked them up and down, drove the car around the block, and returned to confirm Anthony's worst fears. Red said he would do his best. They would need a car to get around in town, and Red offered them a beat up 1940 Plymouth, the same model that Danny Ryan had given him, and directed them to a motel. They stayed two days in Benniston, enjoying grits with eggs each morning. Red got another transmission from a junkyard, installed it for thirty-five dollars, saving their lives and their little holiday. Anthony reflected that this episode would not have ended so well had their breakdown occurred in New York City. Congeniality seemed to characterize his subsequent encounters with people from Georgia. Southern hospitality was not a myth.

At Islamorada Key, Florida, in a motel near the Diving Center, they first met giant southern cockroaches, euphemistically called "water bugs". In no time these were forgotten when they got a rental boat to explore the spectacular coral reefs. The car transmission problems remained long forgotten. One thing disturbed their exhausted sun-induced sleep. The occupant of the next room, a lonely looking obese bone-fisherman, wept and moaned all night, calling out the name of some lost lady friend or wife. In the mornings, he seemed perfectly sane. Recalling his lost Buick lady, Anthony pitied him: he was grateful to have a sensible wife and a reliable car.

The owner of the school paid him for several days as a guide. Each day he speared a grouper to bring to the local diner, which in return gave them free meals, including sublime Key Lime Pie for desert. Anthony met local boys from Marathon and went out in their boat to help spear a twelve-foot hammerhead shark, which struggled endlessly and would not die. They looped its tail and tied it to the stern of the boat: dragging it back ward finally made it stop thrashing. That night they ate fresh shark steak; he also learned that Barracuda, properly cleaned, made good eating. He and Anne gathered coral from the beautiful reef, something that he only later learned, was not a correct thing to do. They put sea fans and brain coral on a plastic sheet in the back seat to take north, thinking, at the time, that this was something like picking flowers or plants and not understanding that they had destroyed an irreplaceable part of a living reef. The decomposing little creatures in the coral smelled so bad that they were forced to stop in Fort Lauderdale for a gallon of Clorox. They soaked the coral, and then spread their ill-gotten treasures in the sun to dry. Almost half a century later, Anthony and Anne kept some of this coral in their home. After seven bright days in the Keys, the Dodge took them back home to the Bronx. The transmission repair done by Red lasted until Anthony traded the Dodge for a new Ford.

A 1957 FORD FAIRLANE

Anthony and Anne kept the Ford known, in its later years as "The Gray Ghost," for ten years. Then his secretary's husband, an orthopedic resident, drove it around Detroit for another two years. This model had a 272 V-8 190 HP engine with "Fordomatic" transmission. Had it not been for the salt and ice that rusted out its body and undersides, the Fairlane could well have gone on forever. The Ford had carried Anthony's family away from their New York roots. During obligatory military service, he and Anne drove south in it, during the midsummer, to Montgomery, Alabama where Anthony was assigned for Air Force orientation, or "Charm School". During that journey, they heard interminable radio broadcasts of the demoralizing beep of *Sputnik*, a miserable satellite that the Russians had placed in orbit, much to the consternation of all Americans. The Fairlane, his first new car, marked a major transition in their lives, along with the height of the Cold War, the beginning of the Space Age, and the ultimate triumph of the space program of the United States.

They had bought the new car, a major step, in the dead of winter of his intern year. He schedule consisted of duty on call all day and every other night and weekend, so Anne's father, a parsimonious, stiff-necked Scotsman, conducted initial negotiations with a New Jersey Ford dealer, supposedly closing what appeared to be a remarkably advantageous deal. But then, for obscure reasons, the arrangement fell apart. Unpleasantness marked Anthony's attempted communications with New Jersey. The dealers were angry, probably because his father-in-law had insisted upon an unreasonable bargain, demanding on an eight-cylinder engine for the price of the standard "Mileage Six". The dealer was singularly unimpressed with Anthony's Dodge trade in.

By the time this family drama and the feud with the New Jersey car dealer reached full height, no one was talking to anyone. Anthony wangled time off from his every other night rotation, drove to New Jersey with the 1949 Dodge and left it with the dealer. He paid the extra $150 that the agency wanted for an eight cylinder engine and drove a Ford from dealer's stock back to their Bronx apartment. On later journeys, he would be grateful for the 190-horse power of its V-8 engine. The Fairlane was one of his better investments. Its tenure marked the first decade of his marriage to Anne, carried him on two long journeys and, ultimately, away from New York City.

The Ford Fairlane, mechanically unique for its era, was at the same time quite stylish. Many of these cars are still around almost half a century later. Fan clubs still abound. The vehicle had a low and sleek silhouette. Standing a little over five feet in height, with a 118" wheelbase, it had a remarkably wide and roomy interior. The front fender assembly extended over the tops of the headlights, giving the appearance, some said, of a partially retracted prepuce. Tasteful tail fins graced its rear. The lower chrome side decorations took a rakish dip amidships, and, given the disputes with the New Jersey Dealer, he settled for the color of a car that they had on the lot, a modest light gray, rather than ordering another new car to be delivered. Dealers always need to get inventory off their lots. The Ford served for house calls during a locum tenens when he did general practice in the Bronx and Yonkers while waiting to begin his mandatory military service. He drove it to Washington DC twice, once to take Part III of the National Board Examinations at Georgetown and later to arrange, successfully, an overseas assignment to a base in Spain. During the time they spent in Spain, the Fairlane remained in his in-laws' garage in Hackensack.

Anthony returned from Spain in the summer of 1960, stopping to retrieve the Ford in New Jersey to drive to the School of Aviation Medicine in San Antonio, Texas where he had been sent to qualify as a flight surgeon. He had gotten his pilot's license and was considering an Air Force career in the accelerating aerospace program, which had, by then, outstripped Russia's efforts. The Ford traveled at an astonishing 85 mph through Missouri where speeds were posted at 80 mph. The car had less than 10,000 miles on the odometer when the right front tire suddenly delaminated causing the car to careen off the road into a ditch. On buying a new tire, the concerned dealer looked at his other tires, which still had plenty of tread. He advised replacing all of them for this high-speed cross-country journey. The dealer measured the remaining tread carefully, giving an honest discount for four new tires. Anthony later thought that this experience might have presaged the tragedies of Ford's Explorers' faulty tires later at the turn of the century.

The car lacked air-conditioning. During the hot Texas summer months none of his new Texas friends would ride in it. This was the time that the Russians shot down Gary Power's U2, Eisenhower denied the existence of our spy program, and Khrushchev pounded on a table with his shoe at the United Nations. The odd part about Khrushchev's outburst was that, in retrospect, the fat old dictator's rage was justified. Anthony's new San Antonio friends, a pair of talented architects, and the County Coroner and his wife, liberal Democrats all, criticized the duplicity of the Eisenhower administration. Anthony thought them effete in complaining about the lack of air conditioning in his Ford, and, given his commitment to the Air Force at a Strategic Air Command base, he considered their views, if not subversive, simply foolish. The U2, Anthony believed, had done no harm, and had given the United States valuable intelligence. His new San Antonio acquaintances, though hospitable and generous, disapproved of his militant view of the cold war and refused to ride in his car. The long hot summer passed quickly. After qualifying as an Aviation Medical Examiner, he drove from Texas to McGuire Air Base, New Jersey in a little over two days. Traveling at night, he slept in air-conditioned motels during the heat of the day and continued on at dusk. His orders demanded a tight schedule in which to get back to his base Spain. He took "go pills", amphetamines, which were then issued to military pilots for long missions.

The Fairlane moved his wife, mother, and son to Detroit in 1962 during his senior surgical residency years; a fortunate move, for he later joined the University faculty. Anne drove the Ford in Detroit, while he drove a 1960 Karmann Ghia, purchased in Spain, and shipped back to the United States courtesy of the United States Air Force. They, like many Americans at that time, had become a two-car family. A great deal happened during the Fairlane years. He began research on sexual dysfunction that attracted international attention, developed a busy surgical practice, and three of their four children were born. The fast reliable Ford took them to the industrial Midwest, where, inevitably, rust got at its body but not its soul.

His first secretary in the Department of Surgery, Carol, was a fine young lady from Plymouth, Massachusetts. She wore her fine straight dark hair about her face like a helmet. The surgeons called her "the little pilgrim". Her husband was an orthopedic resident at the State Hospital and when she left to care for her first baby, she needed a car. Anthony gave her the Fairlane. His chief had been complaining about the ten-year-old rusting Ford in the hospital parking lot. The professor drove a well-polished Detroit-made old style Thunderbird; he had let Anthony know that the eroded

Fairlane in the hospital lot made it look as if his surgical staff was not doing well. Anthony worried about giving the car to Carol as the floorboards had eroded and pavement could be seen below. He had visions of her baby falling through a crack in the floor. Her orthopedist husband, Tony, reconstructed its floor with chicken wire and water resistant plaster, something only an orthopedist would think of. The old Ford graced the Hospital parking lot for two more years while Tony completed training. The chairman continued to grumble about "that wreck", but in a good-natured way. Carol and Tony named the Fairlane "The Gray Ghost". Its plaster floor held while the car took them safely through two long cold winters. They drove it back to Plymouth, Massachusetts, where, Anthony heard, the car went on for two more years.

A 1953 CHEVROLET CONVERTIBLE IN SPAIN

The Air Force suggested that Anthony would need a car for his military assignments at the USAF Hospital in Seville and a Strategic Air Command base, thirty-five miles away at Moron de la Frontera. He would not be able purchase a car in Spain, but the Air Force would ship, at government expense, a "personal vehicle" to Cadiz. The family deemed the Ford too valuable for this venture, and besides, Anne stayed behind in New York for six months and needed the Fairlane. In that summer, he started the search for a used car to ship to Spain. A well-preserved 1953 blue Chevrolet convertible "low rider", now five years old and with abundant shiny chrome, turned up in Brooklyn. He paid cash and drove the car directly to the shipyard with his orders. An amused senior sergeant, on accepting the automobile, commented that, with these wheels, Anthony would have a good time overseas, a prediction that proved to be quite accurate. Among his Spanish friends the car became known as "El Gran Coche Americano"; companions in the First Fighter Day Squadron called it "The Blue Bullet", and the convertible became part of what his Spanish friend, Michel Marques, came to call "La Epoca Grande".

The Air Force accurately predicted his need for a car. Anthony, though he was planning to specialize, became responsible for general surgical and obstetrical care in Seville, some distance from the airbase at Moron de la Frontera, where he billeted in Bachelor Officers' Quarters for six months while awaiting Anne's arrival. General Franco had decreed that air bases be located at least thirty-five miles from cities, then considered to be the radius of destruction of atomic weapons. The base had a few Ford Staff cars, but these, in short supply, were used either by influential noncoms and senior officers.

Two weeks after his arrival, news came that his personal vehicle had arrived in Cadiz. He got orders to proceed directly, in civilian clothing, to pick it up. Uniforms were not allowed off base, as the Spanish insisted that the American military personnel maintain low profiles. Anthony dressed in sport coat and tie. A taciturn motor pool sergeant picked him up at his quarters and drove him south to the ancient seaport in an unmarked blue Ford station wagon. At the dock, he got a sheaf of papers to sign, and then the strange blue convertible was suddenly in his possession. It had virtually no gas in the tank, its tires were semi-flat, but the engine started as soon as they connected the battery cables. As he walked around the car, his driver called out "So long, Doc," flashed an amused grin and drove off. Anthony had been abandoned on a hot August day on a dock in Cadiz, Spain. He had no idea how to ask in Spanish for gas or air for the tires, and now regretted telling personnel officers in Washington DC that he was fluent in Spanish. Gesticulating, he soon established that gas was "petrolio" and good-natured Spanish stevedores waved him to an ancient gas pump on shore. Tires were "pneumaticos"; and air proved to "aire"; he succeeded in getting both of these essentials for the Chevrolet. His next challenge was to get the convertible back to the base. Anthony decided not to stop for lunch.

Only one road ran north from Cadiz, through Jerez, directly through a few little towns and into Sevilla, Once he there he knew the way: over the Guadalquivir River then through Alcala de Quadajiera to the hamlet Moron de la Frontera. He had no road map, and road signs were non-existent on the road from Cadiz. Solemn looking Guardia Civil, with shiny black square cockaded hats, stood at unpaved crossroads. He stopped at each one, identified himself as an Air Force Officer, and received a salute and polite reassurances that he was on the correct route. He drove with the top down, as the air was dry. It would not rain until November, and got back to the Bachelor Officer's Quarters at dusk. Not one Spaniard he encountered spoke English, but rudimentary Spanish, sign language and the intrinsic politeness of the Spanish people sufficed for the journey.

At times, Anthony stayed in Seville with a new friend, Miguel and his wife, Amparrro, for several days or on weekends when clinical duties took him to town. There, he spoke Spanish all the time, and, when he began to dream in Spanish, he had become fluent. Miguel, a Naval Officer, was a civil engineer involved with the construction of the Strategic Air Command base, which harbored B-47 bombers armed with nuclear weapons aimed at targets in the Ukraine. The U2 flights gave them frequent detailed target photographs of military installations. A Tactical Air Command squadron was also stationed at the base, and many of these flyers were frequent passengers in the Blue Bullet. They went to bullfights and explored the surrounding small towns together. The Strategic Air Command Pilots, always on call, never left the base. Miguel and Amparro loved to go out for "paseos" in the convertible on Sunday afternoons. At night, when he could get away, new friends joined by assorted Flamencos cruised around Seville, just as kids did in the United States. The difference was that there were no other cruisers to greet, and these companions sang, clapped and banged on the sides of the car to produce complex contrapuntal flamenco rhythms rather than having a car radio blare rock and roll. They wound through crooked narrow streets, chanting as they passed the Giralda Tower and the house (Casa Pilata) to which Pontius Pilate had retired after serving as Governor of Jerusalem. They sang flamenco about La Casa Pilata,

There amidst the palms and the jalousias, there died Jesu Cristo, of the heat (alli se murio Jesu cristo de la calor que hacia).

Summer days in Sevilla were blazingly hot, but they loved to ride with the top down during the cool summer nights. Later, the base provost told Anthony that that the Air Police and the Guardia Civil knew at all times exactly where they were and what they were doing in the flashy low rider. He found it wondrous to reflect that Pontius Pilate, who had washed his hands of Christ, remained so unpopular centuries later; and that a Chevrolet convertible, driven by a Yonkers kid, rolled over the same cobblestones that Columbus had trod, and upon which countless barefoot penitents had bled. The reality and immediacy of Pilate's house made the story of the crucifixion quite real: for the first time he felt connected to a Christian heritage.

At that time most indigenous cars in Spain were antiques. Spanish mechanics, geniuses at keeping them running, were aided by a dry hot climate ideal for preservation of cars. Gaskets and fan belts tended to dry out and needed frequent replacement, and the mechanics could rebuild or fabricate other parts. His Chevrolet was an older car: the engine needed work and generator needed work. Anthony again found an honest mechanic, Paco, on the outskirts of town near the fabled cigarette factory where Verdi's Carmen had worked. He brought the Chevrolet to Paco's garage, just as it reopened, after siesta at 4:30 in the afternoon. Girls from the nearby factory would walk by the open bay door, on their way back to work just as they did long ago. Paco always had things to say to them, and gradually Anthony's ear became attuned to slang and Paco's broad Andalucian accent. One afternoon, as a beautiful dark haired girl with a stately ass passed by, Paco, in lilting Andaluz, shouted from the bay of his garage,

"If what you have in front is as beautiful as what you have behind I will eat you up!"

The girl smiled, tossed her hair playfully, and continued walking, hips swaying a bit more. They had both been crouched, peering under the hood at the Chevrolet's erratic generator, when Paco suddenly straightened up to sing out this "piropo". The response of New York Irish or Italian girls would have been fearsome. Anthony, amazed, asked him:

"Do you ever actually get anything from that?"

"No" he replied, grinning, "But they really like it; they expect it." This girl deserved the unique compliment and seemed to know it. Paco, then all business, went on to tighten a loosed bracket and fabricate a new part for Anthony's ailing generator.

In October one of Anthony's fighter pilot friends drove with him to Jerez for sherry wine festival. They drank late into the evening; when they went to the men's room for much needed relief, an old lady there who dispensed towels, strained to look at their penises. They became piss shy, retreating to a scraggly thicket across the road to urinate. They later learned that Spanish men were uncircumcised and the old lady simply curious. Spanish men pissed freely, they did not bother going into hiding; instead they discreetly turned their backs to the road. Anthony became comfortable with this custom, a critical requirement after drinking Jerez while consuming salty tapas, as well as a practice possibly good for bladder health.

In January, in time for Three Kings Day, Anne arrived at Cadiz on a boat with a small trunk full of household goods. They rented an apartment in Triana across the Guadalquivir River from the bullring and the Torre de Oro, where treasure from the new world had been stored. A fat lady named

Antonia came to care for them and Anthony's life became orderly once again: no more flamencos or driving around late at night. Ultimately, Anne, in her practical way, convinced him that his precious Chevrolet convertible was too cumbersome for the winding back streets of Sevilla and other Spanish towns. They looked for a small European car and so began another era.

A KARMANN GHIA

A foreigner could actually get a new car in Spain, but it had to be purchased in Tangiers, Morocco and then entered into the country through Gibraltar. This cumbersome arrangement took voluminous paper work and strategic political connections. A used car dealer, a Spanish official and sort of a defunct nobleman, who did this kind of business, had become Anthony's friend. The "count" gladly accepted the 1953 Chevrolet in trade for a blue stylish Karmann Ghia that he billed as a 1960 model, but more likely was a 1959 vintage. Anthony paid for it in advance, sight unseen, and took delivery on a dock in Tangiers, got Spanish papers in Gibraltar, then drove it home to Seville.

This Byzantine negotiation might have seemed a chancy undertaking, but it all went smoothly, and he and Anne had fun in the process. During their several day stay in Tangiers waiting for the car to arrive, they first glimpsed Arab culture, including a bazaar where they haggled for and bought a rug, two camel saddles and a copper coffee table. They toured the destroyed city of Carthage, where the Romans ended the Punic Wars by salting the earth, killing its male inhabitants, and enslaving the rest. Centuries later nothing grew there among the ruins. The result, they were told, was three hundred years of peace called *Pax Romana*. Anthony thought of the B 47's at the base in Moron: the effect of their weapons would have been even more drastic and less likely to bring peace.

A native guide, inevitably named Mohammed, took them to the old town to peer over a parapet into an outdoor courtyard below. Here they saw women slaves chained to walls making the same kind of rugs they had just bought. Their fancy French hotel had a belly dancer; and Anne with Anthony's urging, later tried to imitate her. He ordered, and for the first time, ate Steak Tatar. The waiter had been correctly concerned that this young man did not understand what he had ordered. Fine raw chopped steak is now unavailable, as some busybody will become concerned about eminent death. The Oak Room at the Plaza Hotel in New York, for a while had served steak tartar, and Anthony, whenever he was in New York, always went there for it.

Anthony drove the disguised '59-60 Volkswagen for ten years. The Air Force had shipped it back to New York, and a year later he drove in it, alone, from New York City to Detroit. Its vestigial backbench, barely good enough for small children, was inadequate for adults. In Spain, Miguel Marques had despised the Ghia, mourning the passing of "El Gran Coche Americano." Crammed sideways into in the back seat, Miguel was the picture of misery, but the small coupe was more suitable for European driving. The 1300 cc air-cooled 36 horsepower engine sipped gas lightly, a great advantage as gas stations honoring American Scrip were few and far between.

On weekends, when Anthony could get time off, they drove south to the town of Tarifa, on the Gulf of Algecieras, for spectacular spear fishing. He brought a fresh catch back to the hotel for free meals just as he had done in Florida. After Sunday morning expeditions, they brought a fresh catch back on ice for Sunday night dinner, racing with trucks filled with fish and melting ice for the Monday morning market. They had a modest version of a grand tour in the little car, driving from Spain, east along the Spanish and French Rivieras, south into Italy to see Rome, Naples, Pompeii and returning via the Adriatic side into Venice, then north through Milan, Lake Como, and into Switzerland. They detoured in the south of Italy to visit the town of Anthony's mother's birth, and photographed a fountain she remembered as a child. There were many beggars, people claiming to be relatives flocked around them, kids chanted for "Chick—lees" and, on the road out of town, someone from the side of the road threw grapes at them. He was glad that his family had chosen to immigrate.

Anthony still faced the reality of a fifty-dollar a month income for another three years, so alternate nights, frugally, he and Anne camped out in a tent and other nights they stayed in hotels. At the base in Livorno in Italy where they stopped to purchase gas script, seductive odors from the Post Exchange stimulated an extreme hunger for a hamburger and a chocolate shake. They were, after all, American kids and accustomed to these ways in spite of European Dining experiences. Later, when Anthony was overseas giving lectures or on vacation he would duck into McDonalds in Vienna, Paris and London. In Switzerland, gas stations would not honor US government issued script. The Swiss, rigid, penurious and uncorrupted, would have none of it. On similar principles, Anthony coasted the Ghia in neutral gear down the Eastern Alps into France barely making it to a gas station that accepted US gasoline script.

He had a serious accident with the Ghia. On the drive to the base, the road passed through the hamlet of Alcala de Guadajiera, to become an ill paved main street crowded with trucks, horse drawn carts and people still unaccustomed to the heavy traffic violating their little town. On a rainy winter day, he was driving at the posted 35 speed of km/hr, when a young man darted from behind a truck, passing in the opposite direction, directly into the path of the Ghia. He had no time to stop. Anthony applied brakes, skidded and struck him. The man slid over the roof, and slammed onto the road behind directly behind. His deformed leg was immediately obvious, a closed tibio-fibular fracture which luckily had not broken the skin. A quick examination showed no other injury. A capable corpsman, driving behind him, stopped to help. Together they splinted the limb and carefully put the trauma victim in the back seat of the Chevy station wagon for transport back to the Air Force hospital in Sevilla. Anthony took x-rays, was able to accurately reduce the fracture, applied a long leg cast and consulted the Spanish surgeon who owned the hospital facility next door, renting his second building to the Air Force. The old surgeon, after Anthony paid him, agreed, but not too happily, to attend to the victim's further care.

These actions had been irregular, but the investigating Spanish authorities appeared pleased with the immediate concern for and treatment of this man. Later, several Spanish surgeons gave him gratuitous advice: they would have done an immediate amputation to avoid the long time needed for healing of this type of leg fracture with the aim "to get him back to work". This incident was not to be the last time that Anthony salvaged a leg in spite of advice to amputate.

Grim looking Guardia Civil arrived just after he and the corpsman had completed the fracture reduction and application of a snug long leg cast. Simultaneously, Captain Jay Seaman, of New York, the base attorney also arrived. He looked equally serious. Jay ordered abruptly, in New York accents; "Don'tcha say a word". Then, he turned his attention to the Guardia. Jay did all the talking using voluble Spanish. Anthony went back to work in the clinic, pending a court appearance. The Spanish justice system had been harsh with Americans involved in traffic accidents. Usually there was a fine, jail, and banishment. In this case, their investigation was remarkable for its thoroughness. First, Anthony told his version of the accident to a stern judge. The investigating officers reported that they had measured skid marks to confirm a speed of 35 km/h. Then, to Anthony's surprise, the truck driver who witnessed the incident appeared. He testified that he himself had almost struck the young man. The judge dismissed Anthony with a stern warning, but as the victim's family was poor, Anthony gave them money during the several months this man was out of work. Spanish justice, though autocratic, seemed, at least in this case, to be fair and meticulous. He was fortunate to have been driving the small light Ghia with its streamlined blunt hood and vestigial bumper. The heavy Chevrolet at that speed might have been potentially fatal. Paco, the mechanic next to Carmen's cigarette factory, flawlessly repaired the dented car.

He and Anne brought four children home from the hospital in that little car. His first son was born after trip over a bumpy road in San Pablo, which, apparently induced Anne's labor. The other children three were born at University Hospital in Detroit. The rear mounted VW engine and drive handled the deep Midwestern snows remarkably well. During a freak April snowstorm, he drove back from the Veterans Hospital to Gross Point through three feet of snow in time to take get his wife to the Hospital. One daughter came home on a cool Indian summer's day, and the second in the cold of November. While the VW heater ran off the manifold of an air-cooled engine, the car was always comfortably warm during the winter.

That VW gave promise of going on forever, but then during a particularly rainy year, it constantly failed to start as water moisture accumulated under the distributor cap and other connections. After many unsuccessful efforts to correct this seemingly simple problem, he began carrying a rag and a can of ether, opening the rear engine hood and drying the distributor connections every time it rained. Detroit mechanics seemed unable to solve the moisture problem. It was time for a new car. This time the new car would more colorful and larger than the Ghia. The distributor and all the wiring could have been replaced completely at a VW dealer, but Anthony sensed that the time for change had come. The decision, though delayed, was then made suddenly and virtually on impulse.

A FIAT 124 SPORT SEDAN

Transition from the forth to the fifth decades of life, from the late thirties into middle age at forty, is a dangerous, tumultuous time for most men. And the years 1969 through 1972, when Anthony drove an Italian car, a bright yellow small sedan with a four-cylinder 1200 cc high compression engine, were similarly tumultuous. These years witnessed a sexual and cultural revolution, the onset of the drug culture, the Beatles' invasion, and rebellion against the increasingly bloody, baffling Vietnam Conflict. Dr. Benjamin Spock, the pediatric psychiatrist at Case Western Reserve, marched up Euclid Avenue carrying a Vietcong flag. Though Spock had been his friend and patient, when Anthony got a call from him to join the demonstration, he refused.

The Fiat was a hot little car, thirsty for high-test leaded gasoline. It sported a noisy, poorly muffled exhaust. The stick had five speeds on the floor, and when well tuned, the little sedan accelerated like a rocket. It also had an air horn that sounded like that of a diesel locomotive. That blaring noise could wake the dead, suitable for Italy perhaps, but using it in traffic in an African America neighborhood in Detroit offered the potential to start a riot. He avoided sounding the horn in those areas, though he always blew the claxon as he turned into the driveway of his Gross Point home. His next-door neighbors, the Peabody's who were Boston Brahmins, named the Fiat "The Yellow Peril."

He had driven his tired, beloved Karmann Ghia to a newly established Fiat dealer for the trade in, and then could not bear part with it. A kindly Italian mechanic comforted him,

"It's an old car doc, and you have gotta fugettabbodit". The Fiat had a tape player and suburban kids who rode with him from time to time were surprised to hear *The Lead Zeppelin* and tapes from other Fillmore West performers. While remaining for public consumption a midwestern square, and now 36 years of age, his friends in San Francisco, who did not trust any one over 30, liked him. The tapes were a gift from a young woman, half his age, who could have been his daughter had he sired her in high school days when he owned the rumble seat coupe. The spring of 1970 saw the shootings of students by National Guard troops at

Kent State. That May, the dean dismissed medical school classes for a week. Anthony had been invited to talk at Venice, Italy, and had time to arrange a tour of surgical departments in Rome, Milan and Naples. At the University of Milan, an investigative team trained by Krebs laboratory was examining the same problems in cellular metabolism and diabetes that his laboratory had grants to study. Milanese students had been on strike for months, while the faculty, grateful for their absence, continued their research, recording voluminous and meticulously acquired data in beautifully hand written books. Their findings agreed remarkably well with those of the Detroit laboratory.

All of Italy disapproved of the Vietnam War, and while he had planned to travel by train, a railroad strike made it necessary for him to rent a car. He rented a Fiat 128 with a 1116 cc four cylinder motor that traveled at remarkable speed on autostrada of the Peninsula and handled beautifully on its curved country roads. This performance and the ebullience and hospitality of the Italians strengthened his attraction to these cars. The trip proved to be a happy and exhilarating time. Later that summer, also a bright and happy journey, he drove the Fiat 124 into Canada to explore the lake fishing in the Northern reaches of Ontario. After his return from Ontario, the professor called him in to tell him to get back to work.

Supported by a grant, he began experiments in vascular disease in rhesus monkeys housed in a colony in rural Virginia. The University animal facilities could not yet handle these aggressive creatures. Few clinicians at that time accepted the "cholesterol hypothesis" of vascular disease. As a result of direct observations of arteries, Anthony had become convinced that lowering cholesterol was critical for control of vascular disease. He presented findings of encouraging regressive responses in San Francisco and Italy and whenever he could, but was disappointed with the lukewarm silence that greeted his observations. Even his wife, Anne, was publicly skeptical.

At that time, laboratory values for serum cholesterol of 250 to 300mg/dl were accepted as normal in humans. His group found that vascular disease progressed in animals at these same modest levels. It seemed obvious to him that cholesterol lowering needed to be incorporated into clinical practice. But the skeptics required endless iterations of the same research. As his laboratory got national funding support and his surgical practice became increasingly popular, women appeared offering to help him. Some truly wanted to help and others offered propositions to become a mistress, a muse or both. The pill had newly liberated the women of the 70's, and society had yet to encounter the downside of promiscuity in the form of immune deficiency disease, which was lurking, nonetheless, in Africa. A vivacious French woman, who drove a Corvette and had inherited a boat called *a Bientot,* told him that wives were acceptable; she wanted him as he was. But she would not tolerate another girlfriend. She turned out to be so demanding of time that "a bientot" was a convenient way to say goodbye before any thing much developed. One blonde promised, when he told her that he was married, that she would never ask for Saturday night or Sunday, but quickly broke that promise. He became so busy that the time and energy to accept or act upon these offers, however tempting, became burdensome. One woman wanted to drive south to Sandusky where some motels featured pornographic films on closed TV circuits and seemed to be particularly interested in scenes of double penetration. The advent of motels made the need to park in cars obsolete. Professional success in middle age brought danger and temptation, but he found it better to drive a flamboyant car than to have an affair. Anne's patience with his automotive foibles helped considerably.

His group had promulgated a diet low in cholesterol, saturated fat, and refined sugars, which received public attention, as such advice, bordering on a fad, still does. The diet banned eggs, which was likely wrong, dairy products, and red meat, which might also have been, to a degree, incorrect in its rigor. Anthony, with this rebellion against conventional diets, had a captive audience and attracted true believers among Vietnam era medical students. Three student Weathermen came to his office after one of his lectures. They volunteered to undertake a holy mission, stamping out cholesterol by blowing up chicken coops all over the Michigan Peninsula. At first thinking, that they were joking, he was amused. The prospects of exploding chicken feathers and feces seemed funny; he then realized that these young men were deadly serious. Their zeal was genuine, but he talked them out of this radical venture to ensure public health. One of them later went to jail, but after serving two years, their liberal medical school dean readmitted him to medical school. This Weatherman, Anthony later heard, became a conservative Republican practicing rural Michigan.

These were heady times, but after two years, everything in the Fiat made of plastic began to fail: light switches, windshield wiper controls, inner door handles, in short, anything that protruded from the dash or the steering column. Even the knob on the gearshift fell off. With regular maintenance by the dealer, the incandescent Italian car performed beautifully, but the acronym for FIAT, "Fix It Again Tony" held true. He quickly tired of these nuisances and the car much sooner than he ever had before, as colorful toggle switches continued to fall from the dash, dangling by thin wires, even as one after the other was replaced.

In late 1972, Anthony got a call from a frightened father, the owner of a Dearborn Buick Dealership. His daughter, a freshman at Toledo, had just called him from the student clinic there. She complained of an acutely swollen leg that began after sitting cross-legged in tight jeans and smoking with her friends. She had been told, her father said, that she would require anticoagulants and that she would be disabled for life with a swollen leg. Anthony arranged her transfer and got her into the operating room within four hours. In the preoperative area, the distraught father confided that his daughter, a freshman, had begun dating senior at Maumee, who had convinced her to take birth control pills. The father told him, piteously, that nothing had happened yet: she had not yet had sex. Now that Anthony had daughters, he understood the father's vain hope perfectly. While prepping her for operation, the marks of tight jeans, which had compressed her vein, were still evident in her groin. Using local anesthesia, his team exposed the common femoral vein; he made a transverse incision, and had her cough vigorously. A clot immediately extruded from the iliac vein above, and they were able to massage more clots from below. They sutured the opening in the vein avoiding the use of forceps and clamps and gave her a heparin infusion for a week. An x-ray later showed completely normal veins;

fortunately, the blood clot had been removed before it could stick to the vein walls. The grateful father offered Anthony the gift of any Buick in his inventory. Tongue in cheek, Anthony described an air-conditioned yellow convertible with black upholstery. A month the dealer called to tell him that a special order had arrived at the dealership.

A 1972 BUICK CONVERTIBLE

That spring Anthony went to see the car the owner of the Buick agency had ordered. The custom Skylark Convertible, color code Y was billed as sunburst yellow, with black bench seats, turbo hydra-matic transmission, and a sandalwood ragtop. A 350 cubic inch V8 engine with a 4-barrel carburetor supplied power. The air-conditioning and heating effectively formed a climate bubble with the top down and windows up. The dealer even got him vanity plates: this car became ADA 1. The Skylark later moved to Nevada by truck, and came eventually to Maryland to be driven by his children. He finally was sold it in 1984 for $3,500; just what Anthony had insisted on paying for it. The dealer wanted to give him the car. While Anthony appreciated this offer, he had his surgical corporation bill for the procedure and paid exactly the dealer's invoice charge for the special order.

The years of the yellow cars were colorful, but in many ways troubled and sad. Richard Milhous Nixon was elected in 1968; the war in Vietnam then expanded. Young men marched in Washington chanting "Hell no, we won't go", but his preoccupied life as a busy surgeon shielded him from political awareness or substantive opinions about global or national issues. He and his suburban friends, conservative Republicans, remained content to lead an unexamined life. In spite of rumors about Watergate, it seemed not a bad thing when Nixon won a landslide election in 1972. Then, the national scene deteriorated even more.

During this time, he became involved with competitive sailing in summer and skiing in the winter, when Lake St Claire had frozen over. His old fashioned chief had rigidly maintained the institution of Saturday morning grand rounds. In a constant rush on Saturdays to get to one o'clock racing starts at the Yacht Club, he began to garner speeding tickets. A homicide detective, the son of one of his patients, gave him a gold police badge to keep with his car registration. This reduced his point accumulation, provided he had the foresight display the badge before the officer started writing a citation. He told the police the truth about where he was going, that is mostly to sailboat races. The yellow convertible was not only woman magnet; it was also a police magnet.

At home in Gross Point, lived four children, his wife, Anne, his mother, five Siamese cats, and a dog, which could not pass obedience training nor it could travel in his car without being sick. These were such busy times, filled with doing and doing and with little time for introspection. At dinner every night, he marveled at his crowded table. Where did all these people come from? The family cars, driven by his wife after the Ford Fairlane were a Ford Galaxy, then a Buick from the same dealer who ordered the Skylark. This time, he had to negotiate strenuously for a favorable price for the second Buick, canceling his original order and ordering a car from a competing dealer before the first Buick agency called him to offer a lower price. One charity from a dealership was apparently enough, and he had been left solely in the hands of a floor salesman.

After the death of his father in law, Anne and her mother bought Ford Victorias, terrible cars that, for inexplicable reasons, stalled. These Fords had erratic complicated carburetors that no one could adjust, presaging bad times for Ford Motors. During this era, Henry Ford II did some remarkably stupid things not only in Detroit but elsewhere. Besides birthing the Edsel, he fired Lee Iocacca and other top executives, promoted Thomas McNamara, gave Ford's body processing operations at Dearborn to the Japanese, and ran around with women to the extent that he failed to pay attention to business. After the Ford Victorias, Anthony's family bought no more Fords. McNamara went on to mastermind the Vietnam War, strategizing with bean and body counting. Much later he wrote a terrible book apologizing for it all. While systems approaches seemed work for particular engineering solutions, Anthony found that misguided people in leadership positions thought that "systems engineering" could make them infallible. Anthony developed a deep distrust of this genre, which was just beginning to impact medical practice.

So much happened during the kaleidoscopic years of the yellow cars. His surgical department started practice as a corporation, and as treasurer and director, he sat at the feet of a senior accountant from the nearby firm of Ernst and Whinny. Anthony learned elementary corporate law and governance from an attorney who, arguing before the Supreme Court, had won physicians' groups the right to incorporate. His sailing skills at the Detroit Yacht Club progressed from miserable performances in a small one-design, to winning ways in a Cal 29, with a Dutch sailor who taught him much and then on to a partnership, with the owner of Tartan Marine, in a remarkably fast light 44 foot sloop. They won major races in the Atlantic and Caribbean. Sailboats seemed to attract a certain type of woman even more than flashy cars. Willing girls were always hanging around them in port. They called these girls "mostly's", when asked where they lived, some of these poor groupies replied, "Mostly in sail bins." Once in port after distance races, Anthony immediately left the boat and never slept aboard. Before going ashore to a hotel, he announced the precise time they were to sail again. When he returned, below decks sometimes smelled like hemp, but by the time he boarded, the girls were standing on the dock and the crew was ready to sail. His crew was so good that he made no comments about what they might choose to do in port. And the crew always told the girls, "The ship always sails." An old infantry sergeant in the National Guard had once told Anthony, "If they don't fuck they don't fight." This seemed true in competitive sailing as well. That crew pulled mightily on every halyard and sheet. When their sailing triumphs, extraordinary accomplishments for a boat of Midwestern origin, made *Sports Illustrated* and the local papers, his boss, the old school surgeon commented, "If you don't put away that boat and get to work you'll never amount to anything."

Responsibilities for research kept him busy, and case after case of vascular procedures needed to be done. They found that smoking, rather than cholesterol level, was the major factor causing early clotting of bypass grafts. Not long after, President Carter fired his secretary of Health and Human services for recommending smoking cessation. Amidst those kaleidoscopic times, many helped him succeed with his work. Three steadfast laboratory assistants, Angela from Dearborn, a passionate poetess of lights and fires, edited his writings; Dorothy, a radical and pacifist from San Francisco helped at the start then left, inexplicably, to marry a high ranking Republican official; a pair of bohemian African explorers in Virginia managed their first primate colony; and senior scientists in pathology, medicine and surgery guided him, tempering his inherent impatience.

Surgical colleagues stimulated his lifelong interest in surgical outcomes research and encouraged his technical innovations in the surgery of male erectile dysfunction. One of his crew, later a Vice President at Morgan Stanley, helped invest their corporate pension funds prudently and profitably. The yellow cars took him and his family unfailingly to an Episcopal parish each Sunday, where he thanked God for personal blessings of that time and asked for forgiveness of his sins.

Invitations to surgical departments to be considered for a chairmanship began to come. Some of the places that

wanted him, he did not want, and others that he might have
wanted, did not choose him. He coveted the Chair in
Detroit, but the local search committee did not want an
insider or one associated with his old fashioned chief. Anthony
was politically naïve and made enemies by being outspoken,
but one position caught his fancy, that of Chairman at a
new medical school in Nevada.

Two years after he got the Skylark, on August 9th 1974,
Richard Nixon was forced to resign over the Watergate
scandal, and Anthony registered as a Democrat to vote in
the primary for John Glenn. An honest Midwesterner,
William Ford, served as president, then lost to Jimmy Carter
in 1976 over a silly remark about Poland. Then, the gas
shortage struck the nation followed by an economic crisis
with spiraling interest rates. At that time, Anthony began to
ride a motorcycle to work, but his insurance agent called at
his home to upbraid him. Soon after, the Kawasaki was stolen
from his driveway; even Motown suburbs far from the ghetto
were not secure. His mother had to go to a nursing home
with Alzheimer's disease, but the Carter years' high interest
rates just supported her small retirement fund until she died.

By fall of 1979, the glamorous Yellow Skylark had been
ravaged by salt and brutal Midwestern winters. After
replacing three ragtops, he had the body rebuilt down to
the rocker panels and that winter stored the convertible in a
garage. In spite of his Fiat experience, he then bought another
Italian car, a Lancia. Love, some say, is the suspension of
disbelief. In 1979, the refurbished Skylark and the new
Lancia went by truck to Nevada. The Iran Crisis loomed
and was not helped by President Carter's hesitant handling,
but then, the young US Olympic Hockey team became

world champions. This gave Russia and the rest of the world something to think about. Somehow, the decade of the yellow cars ended safely.

A 1979 LANCIA SEDAN

Anthony had not yet been cured of his Italian affection, more properly affectation. He had heard that the Lancia, an upgrade from the Fiat, was truly "la bella machine". When the time came to put the Skylark away after its rescue from rust, he leased a 1979 Lancia sedan, with a high compression engine and power train much like that of the Fiat. The upscale dealer assured him that none of the switches would fall out and promised excellent maintenance. This held true in Motown where, faithfully, he took the car to an Italian garage on the outskirts of town for tune-ups and oil changes by Milanese mechanics. The four-cylinder engine also ran an air conditioner, but not too well, and the car had a tape deck. He spent peaceful afternoons at the shop, smoking de Nobili cheroots with the men while they serviced, fussed with valves and fine-tuned the Lancia's powerful little engine.

The Lancia coincided with a time for another change. That year, he traveled west to Reno and Las Vegas to consider the Chairmanship of Surgery at the University of Nevada. His chief had to retire. They were to have a new chairman, but the choice would not be him or any in his department. He made about five trips in all, including Anne, his youngest son Francis, his laboratory staff and corporate office manager. Ultimately, he accepted the position, and in the spring of 1980 moved to Nevada. John Higgins, the talented African-American laboratory assistant, packed the laboratory and came west with him. They sent equipment and furnishings along with the Lancia in a large van. The dean had given them permission to move critically needed laboratory equipment purchased with his grants, including an ultracentrifuge and an EMU 3G electron microscope to the new medical school. A line formed at the door of the laboratory to scrounge whatever was left over, but Mr. Higgins, six feet six and 290 pounds, guarded and packed all their precious equipment and saw to it that it was safely loaded. Their precious colony of dogs and rhesus monkeys with vascular disease were shipped separately. Without John, the move might have resembled the scene in the death of *Zorba the Greek*.

That year the Lancia's tape deck played Billy Joel and the Beatles. In Nevada, at the suggestion of the acting surgical chair, a slender surgeon who wore cowboy clothing, he hosted a meeting of the local Surgical Society. After dinner at a fancy Italian restaurant, the waiter handed him a bill for $1250, while about twenty-five surgeons watched, poker faced, for his reaction. Anthony paid the bill without comment. Exiting the parking lot, the cowboy surgeon turned and told Anthony that he was now a member of the Reno Surgical Society. His hosting of the dinner comprised his initiation. After this night, there would be about thirty dinners, one each month, each hosted by different members. For the price of entry, the dinners, the fine times and camaraderie, his investment paid great dividends. These evenings started with cocktails and bawdy jokes, followed by a scientific presentation, and a gourmet dinner. Each surgeon tried to outdo the other in selecting the best restaurant and menu. At first, only one or two young women attended, but later members began to invite the increasing numbers of female medical students. Meetings got tamer and tamer and jokes more insipid, until the ribaldry altogether stopped. Later, as the society grew, their meetings again became elegant, albeit refined, but possibly less informative scientifically. Two or three on call surgeons were not allowed to drink, but they usually showed up. Nevada State Troopers monitored these affairs and they were tough on DUI, whether or not miscreants were professional men.

Anthony had cared for an English Professor from University of Nevada. Tongue in cheek, the professor commented that his move, given the Silver State's rakish reputation, "Might seem to be a chancy and parlous undertaking." Anne and her mother certainly felt that way, given Nevada's colorful past. But then, her family had disapproved of their move to Spain, somehow implying that he was moving their only daughter to Spanish Harlem. Experience demonstrated, in both instances, that he had made the right choice. In a formal final interview, the University Vice President, also an English Professor, told Anthony that he knew nothing about surgery and, instead, quizzed him about Chaucer. The University did not lack intellectual horsepower.

On the night he flew to Nevada, he went directly to a picturesque cottage on Newlands Circle, in old Reno. The dean had arranged a rental with an option to buy the unique dwelling. The Shiny Lancia, with Michigan Plates ADA 2, had been unloaded and parked in a breezeway surrounded by a well-kept garden. The housekeeper had unpacked his belongings and made up a bed. The house reflected the "Biggest Little City's" intimate atmosphere. A skilled architect had it built in the style of a French provincial cottage for his wife in memory of their honeymoon in the South of France. It had a thatched roof, cut glass leaded casement windows, fine timbers, and a large fireplace. This home appeared as a feature in *Architectural Digest*. The woman, Betsy, who had lived there, loved the cottage, but as Anthony soon found, she also haunted the place.

On his first night in town, although he had hotel reservations, he decided to sleep in the cottage. The MGM hotel, where he had reservations, called awakening Anthony. When he failed to appear, the night manager had become concerned for his safety, as newcomers to Nevada's wild ways often found ways to get into trouble and hotel-casino managers prided themselves on caring for their guests. After reassuring the manager, and with the time change, he again fell into a deep sleep, and then his Siamese cat, Mali Ying Kitti, began to yowl and cry. He awoke at 1AM to the sounds of footsteps on the cottage's creaky floors. He found that disturbances appeared when the house was untidy, as on that first night Anthony learned that the former mistress of the cottage had died unexpectedly at that hour at a nearby hospital. Her surgeon, a highly capable man, never understood her death. He had performed emergency, though uneventful operation for an inflamed colon that he had almost completed when she arrested.

The next day, he drove the Lancia downtown to find a bank. He was driving slowly, hesitantly navigating one-way downtown streets and peering into noisy casinos that opened virtually onto the street, when a pair of Nevada troopers pulled him over. One got out of the car. After polite inquiries, they gave him precise directions on how to negotiate the peculiar one-way downtown streets without making illegal turns. Two weeks later, while at home alone in the cottage having a quiet dinner, the doorbell rang. The same trooper, looking quite official, was standing at his front door. He greeted him pleasantly as Doctor DeAngelo. He seemed to know about his new position and status, and offered him, quite seriously, congratulations upon becoming a Nevadan. Then, the trooper reminded Anthony that it was now time for the Lancia to have Nevada license plates. His new office manager, originally from Oklahoma, went to the DMV for the license plates the next day and got them, just as she did everything, quickly and efficiently. The Lancia now had Nevada's silver and blue plates, ADA 2. Later, when the Skylark arrived by truck to be driven by his son, Francis, the police quickly noticed Ohio plates and stopped him as well. He promptly mounted Nevada plates on the Buick too.

Little passed unnoticed in the "Biggest Little City". At a dinner honoring new medical faculty at a district judge's home, the issue of the brothels arose. One of the faculty wives was complaining bitterly, whining about their legal status. The judge's wife, an attractive lady from an "Old Reno Family" addressed the table,

"When we came west in covered wagons, few women cared to make the journey. These houses were legal then and they are now. They are the right of every western man."

She meant her remarks to be taken seriously. Her family had come west in covered wagons and these pioneer women loved the west. It was true also that many Eastern women hated the western environment, particularly Nevada, with its personal freedom to gamble and, if one chose, to whore around. Anthony's family had stayed behind to sell the Gross Point home, and he was to remain, in this provocative environment, a temporary bachelor for almost year. The judge added, pointedly directing his remarks to Anthony,

"But Doc, if you move a woman into your place we will know about it on Court Street tomorrow morning."

Anthony drove the the Lancia for rounds starting at 5:30 AM; first to St Mary's Hospital downtown, then to Washoe Hospital, south across the railroad tracks, and then to the Veterans Hospital where he spent the rest of the day with students, residents, and Nevada Veterans, a special breed of men. At dawn, he sped south to beat the morning train that stopped, every morning, in the center of town, blocking its main street. The inconvenience did not bother him. Some thought that, according to lore, every true western town needs a train stopping in its center, so that a lonely stranger could get off. Anthony imagined himself the lonely stranger, but this soon changed. He came to love the town and its straightforward people, quickly acquiring a circle of friends.

One of them, a lantern jawed Irishman, the broker for his group's corporate pension fund, became a loyal companion. He and Jimmy O'Neill had a kind of contest. One night he cooked supper in the cottage, and the next night, Jimmy paid for dinner at one of the Casinos or local Basque restaurants. It turned out that the stockbroker was right: it was cheaper to eat out in Nevada than to cook at home. Inevitably, women came to the cottage on one pretext or another, but the confirmed bachelor and misogynist, got rid of them with a few caustic remarks. Jimmy had had a bad experience in New York and distrusted virtually all women. Every week or two, he put on a lumber jacket to visit the Mustang Ranch, passing himself off a truck driver. This strategy was, like his dinners, less expensive and possibly more convenient than dating or marriage. Their pension fund steadily grew under Jimmy's critical direction.

The university surgical service grew busier and busier. At 6:30 each Wednesday morning after rounds, he drove to the airport to fly 400miles south to Las Vegas, where his Vice Chairman and a talented local fracture surgeon had developed an outstanding trauma and burn service. Anthony spent weekends at Lake Tahoe, to get his Tartan ten-meter sailboat tuned and sails adjusted to perform at an altitude of almost 6000 feet above sea level. This required recutting the sails and less rigging tension so that they displayed a deeper curve and more billow than at lower altitudes. That summer, crewed by an inexperienced but willing bunch of desert rat medical students, the boat won the trans-Tahoe race. The crew was led by an expert Finn sailor, a transplant from Santa Monica, California, who drove them mercilessly and later went on to become an outstanding cardiac surgeon.

While the high desert air agreed with his sailboat, the more modest altitude of the Washoe Valley did not agree with "la bella machine". The Lancia's engine became progressively balky. Anthony took it to several shops in town, but found no one who could get it to run smoothly. The engine missed and lost power. The car could barely climb the Sierra to the Tahoe slip at Sunnyside. In many vain attempts, he left the car at one shop after the other. In one of them, the radio and tape deck were stolen and the engine still missed and lost power.

Three years had passed, and the lease for the Lancia ended. Anthony called Detroit to tell the rental agency that he was done with the car. The agency did everything they could to get him to buy it. He resisted, knowing there was no one in Reno who could tune that engine which required periodic valve adjustments. One theory attributed the deteriorating performance to "soft" exhaust valve seats. "Hardened" seats were installed in most domestic engines by the mid-seventies to compensate for the federally mandated removal of lead from gasoline. Without the lead additive, soft valve seats progressively receded and no longer sealed effectively. In early spring, the agency sent a tentative vague woman who appeared to be a recycled hippy from San Francisco to drive the Lancia over the Sierra. She arrived at Newlands Circle late and started her journey in the afternoon; not heeding warnings that getting snowed in on the mountain was possible as late as April or May. The Lancia's engine was missing and losing power badly. Anthony followed her in the Skylark to the top of Donner Pass. Once over the 7000-foot summit, it was down hill slide to San Francisco where "la bella machine" might find an Italian mechanic and a happier life.

A 1982 MERCEDES TURBODEISEL

The chief of medicine and Anthony decided to buy new cars at the same time, but they both worried that their purchases would be viewed as ostentatious. People in academic medicine who drove expensive cars attracted criticism. Anthony had trouble understanding this concern. A few private medical practitioners flaunted expensive vehicles and likely, most of them including academicians, worked as hard as corporate executives who drove luxury vehicles. Between them, they decided upon the 350 Mercedes turbodeisel. Anthony made the arrangements to purchase the car in Klamath Falls, Oregon for a little less than $30,000. A surgical colleague flew him up to the pretty little town in his Cessna. After being warned about the hazards running out of fuel in a diesel car, he filled its tank, buckled his seat belt, and drove the Mercedes south east out of the green Oregon countryside and into the dun colored Nevadan desert. This was the first time he used a seat belt: a sailing partner and orthopedic surgeon who treated trauma, had severely criticized him when he drove unbelted to San Francisco for winter regattas. He arrived in Reno by nightfall.

The Mercedes was his first luxury car, but there had been compromises. The seats were vinyl rather than leather and the 350 was not the top of the model line. But once the turbo kicked in, the car accelerated well on the highway. The motor sounded terrible when idling, producing a dreadful odor. That 350 model handled a bit like a tank; later he learned that the Germans nicknamed it "Der Panzer Wagon". It hated the hills of San Francisco and performed badly on snow and ice. When the temperature dropped below freezing, starting the engine became a serious problem. Once again, he carried ether to pour in the air intake for those occasions. After he had moved to east, he got stranded in Princeton, New Jersey in winter with a dead battery. He had been invited to give grand rounds there, and had left the lights on overnight. The tow truck operator commented, as he gunned the trucks generator, that it took the New Jersey power grid to get the diesel engine to turn over.

In spite of his love for the Silver State, he had accepted the offer of Chair of Surgery at a University in the Nation's capital. Anne quickly packed and moved with enthusiasm, leaving Nevada to arrive in Washington in time for their daughters to start the school year in September. John Higgins and Anthony followed later in the fall, driving the turbodeisel across the country. Its trunk contained valuable etchings and their laboratory records. Jesus Cortez, "Chucho", an earnest young Mexican, who worked for a local judge, had volunteered to come. At the last minute, although Chuco had a visa, he changed his mind, fearing that Washington DC might itself be the "*gran migra*", an even bigger immigration service. Although he was a legal immigrant, he feared that, in some way he would be found wanting and be sent back to Mexico. His fears were unfounded. Actually, immigration enforcement was much tougher in Nevada than on the East Coast. Chucho remained behind looking after the cottage, continuing his education, and ultimately becoming a United States citizen. Cucho's hesitation proved fortunate because the house took a long time to sell, and he continued as its caretaker. Anthony went back twice to Reno, walking the grounds while they both wept, recalling the parties there with the medical students and surgical residents. This had been, like the Andalucian time, another *epoca grande*.

Early on the morning of their journey, just east of Reno on Route 80, they passed a hodgepodge of buildings on the Truckee riverbank, an iron gated complex comprising the Mustang Ranch. Anthony commented,

"Well, John, that's the last time we'll ever see that".

Higgins replied abruptly,

"They don't let us in there anyway." Anthony had not realized until then that the Mustang Ranch was strictly segregated. John's angry response surprised him. Ordinarily an amiable companion, Higgins reminded him of old low-key friends in the Bronx and Yonkers. They had a tradition of attending Detroit Tigers baseball games together.

The seven-day drive had been planned to see some the country. A Nevada medical student had, in glowing terms, described the grandeur of a cross-country automobile journey. The student had been quite correct, the drive proved to be a spectacular experience. Anthony and John encountered a bit of unpleasantness. On the second day, stopping at a bar for lunch somewhere in middle of Wyoming, two old looking cowboys and a grizzled bartender turned to glare as they entered. Sensing overt hostility, Anthony felt that something needed to be said. Grinning, he said lightheartedly,

"Well, here is trouble if you are looking for it." Then he put on his nasty Italian scowl. John, standing 6'6" and weighing 290 pounds, stood glowering beside him. The bartender quickly looked down into the sink, and the cowboys, just as quickly, turned their attention back to their beers. A skinny waitress, face wreathed in smiles and wrinkled sun-damaged skin, gave them juicy rare hamburgers. They ate quickly, not pressing their luck, then continued the drive east on route 80.

On crossing the Great Divide, the landscape turned from the dun tan of the west to dark green. After a steak dinner in Omaha, they stayed in the same roadhouse for the night. In the morning, in Iowa, turning off the great highway on a whim, they drove twenty-five miles north on a secondary road to a small farm town, where a spirited baseball game was in progress in progress. They got out of the car to watch.

Hefty looking men and women in bib overalls invited them to the home team dinner. The Iowan's seemed pleased to have Anthony and John for fans, so they stayed for two days, as cheerleaders for the hometown team, which won the little series. Then they pressed eastward through Chicago, detouring north and getting to Detroit by nightfall. John visited his family and Anthony visited the Peabody's in Gross Point, for a day of rest, superb meals, and good conversation with old friends. Their final drive took them from Detroit to Bethesda, Maryland by late afternoon where Anne had rented a home.

En route, somewhere in the middle of rural Ohio on a hot humid afternoon, they both managed to cause a stupid accident. Higgins had gotten more and more morose at the prospect of leaving their high desert homes and the crisp Sierra air. They had stopped for gas on route 80, to make a pit stop, and to switch drivers. When Anthony returned from the rest room, his companion sat slouched in the passenger's seat, glumly staring out the window. Higgins said nothing, but he had the gas hose attached to the tank. Anthony's bad mood mirrored his Higgins's apathy. Impatiently, Anthony started to drive away, ripping the hose from the pump, and damaging the Mercedes' gas tank. Ohio State Troopers came, sizing up what they thought might be an unsavory pair, and decided to make a big deal of the incident. Anthony took total responsibility for the mishap so they avoided jail for reckless driving. Later, Allstate Insurance wanted to raise his insurance premiums astronomically. Once he got a new connection for the gas tank, Anthony cancelled his Allstate policy. This had been the first claim that he or his family had submitted in over three decades. Apart from this costly misadventure, the total bill for diesel fuel for that journey was seventy-six dollars. The Panzerwagon, though far from glamorous, proved to be a prudent investment.

Early on a steamy September morning, Anthony and John drove east on Canal Road into the District of Columbia. Although September can be a fine month in Washington, that day was hot and humid. The overhang of Kudzu over the Canal road gave them the sensation of driving into a swamp. This impression was correct: most parts of central Washington, DC were reclaimed low-lying swampland. In spite of the University's generous offer to hire John to manage its research laboratories, John felt that, were he to move DC, he would be back in the ghetto again. He returned as an EEO officer for the University of Nevada.

During the steamy Washington summers, the air conditioning in the Mercedes began to malfunction. It turned out that these vehicles, after importation, were outfitted with Chrysler Motors equipment. Then, after five years, the transmission needed a series of repairs, which at the dealership were inordinately expensive. Anthony began journeying to a small cluttered shop on Georgia Avenue that specialized in Mercedes repairs for impecunious Mercedes Cognoscenti who enjoyed the prestige of the car but balked at the expense.

Anthony kept the original Oregon plates in the District for more than a year, not having the time to get new ones. Finally, he dedicated a morning at the Motor Vehicle Bureau in the District to get license plates reading ADA 3. He parked the car out front, in metered parking, thinking that this process would take an hour. Some of the people in the long line, mostly African Americans, recognized him from their visits to city clinics that he attended. They insisted on getting him to the front of the line, so he escaped without a parking ticket, and finally obtained DC plates.

Neither the car nor the Oregon plates had escaped notice in the hospital parking lot. Nobody bothered about out of state plates, which were ubiquitous in the District. Washington, though not a big town, seemed in many ways much less organized than the "Biggest Little City" in northern Nevada. His Dean commented, with a hint of envy and sarcasm in his tone, that Anthony's white Mercedes looked exactly like a German taxicab. He predicted that its automatic windows would get stuck when it rained. The windows never malfunctioned, but other things, some good others quite bad, happened during the time of the Mercedes and his tenure that troubled institution.

Anthony's collaborator and friend, John Higgins, died while he was away lecturing in India. He failed to get back to Detroit for John's funeral and, once again, regretted never having the chance to say goodbye to an old friend. Financial problems plagued the hospital: faculty unrest about compensation became a continual issue. There seemed to be no end to whining and complaining, including the dismal traffic reports barraging television screens and radios each morning. Used to driving in snow, he hated the way the city reacted to shut down after any minor snowfall. The Dean's sarcasm about expensive cars was an omen of bad things to come. He missed Nevada and its Western ways, where win or lose, people rarely bragged, explained, or whined. He made no secret about his preference for these ways over the endless second-guessing of Washington. This attitude did not win many friends.

INFINITI Q45 1990

Once Anthony made the decision to discard an old car and buy a new one, he acted without delay. In this instance he decided to give up the Mercedes turbodeisel only after considerable deliberation. In spite of its shortcomings, once he found the frugal mechanic on Georgia Avenue, the Panzerwagon threatened to go on, with all its annoyances, forever. He had driven the car for eight years and had tired of its quirks, its noise, its smell; its rough diesel idling and balky starts in cold weather. The radio had developed an irritating habit of malfunctioning in hot weather and the turbo, for some obscure reason that the mechanic could never find, did not regularly kick in during highway driving. This break up was prolonged; his search for a new car was slow and deliberate.

Now in his fifty's, Anthony decided that he would buy the very best new car he could for his tedious drives from the suburbs into the District. He test-drove, in quick succession, a Jaguar XKE V12 convertible, pre-owned by a failed building contractor, a Cadillac Seville, and the new 350 Lexus sedan. A fellow surgeon, enthusiastic about the Jaguar, had just purchased a new XKE, in the belief that this car would eventually become valuable as a collectors item. Every time his sleek convertible was turned left, its horn sounded and this almost always marked his entry into medical center garage, which required a series of left turns. The Jaguar enthusiast had difficulty getting this bizarre malfunction corrected; his only consolation was that the horn did not sound during the series of right hand turns needed to exit the parking area. Anthony test-drove the contractors XKE with only 3000 miles on it around Rockville and lower Maryland. The car had been stored in the contactors unused shed and was speckled with bird droppings. The wind noise with the top up was loud; the long car had the turning radius of a truck, and required 17 seconds from a stop to reach 60 mph. The Cadillac seemed somehow unprepossessing, almost a cliché of its former glory. The Lexus appeared interesting, but driving in it felt like being suspended within an isolated box with no connection to the road. Its interior resembled that of his wife's old Toyota Cressida.

A love affair began during the last day of the auto show in March 1990 at the DC convention center. A beautiful cream-colored sedan, a Q 45 Infiniti, was spotlighted on a dais far in the back of the hall. A reserved low-key salesman told him described its unique features. The next day Anthony drove the same remarkable car on a winding road in Northern Virginia. The test drive settled it. A righteous love struck once more. He negotiated a five-year lease for a total of $38,000 from the Infiniti Dealer and the wondrous Q car, one of the earliest sold in Virginia, with its 340 HP V8 engine became his with license plates ADA 4 in DC, and later, ADA 4 in Nevada. Anthony never regretted his choice, and the love affair lasted twelve years. When the lease expired after five years, he was again living in Nevada, so he took it to a reputable luxury car dealer who advised him, in contrast to the situation with the Lancia, to buy the Q for the residual $18,000, assuring him that he would not get a better bargain anywhere.

People that rode with him in that car came to love it. One of his colleagues, a prominent California surgeon, was so taken with the Q that he bought two, one for his wife and one for himself. However, the later models were sold with a 278 HP V6 engine. With the larger engine, he drove the Q in third gear in town to keep the revolutions at about 1500-2000 per minute. The powerful engine proved to be an important asset during two transcontinental trips. In the spring of 1994, he again went west back cross-country to become a dean at the Nevada medical school and chief at a federal hospital. Then, the fall of 2000, he drove his Q from Nevada back to Washington to assume a post in Health and Human Services. On these drives, people in the small towns where he stopped to refuel came to look under the hood. Anthony learned the pleasure of a long journey in a fine machine, enjoying high speed performance, listening to tapes, and free from worry about breakdowns.

On his first drive west, after a night in Grand Junction, and a spectacular morning journey through the Arches Park Desert, the Infiniti glided into shining Salt Lake City. The journey next day, from Salt Lake to Reno, took only ten hours, the Q45 clocking 140 miles an hour at 5000 rpm on straight stretches. When he purchased this car, the Virginia dealer had recommended adding a spoiler on the trunk. Anthony wished that he had accepted this offer. A spoiler on a sedan, Anthony thought might be an affectation, but at the high speeds so easily achieved in the desert, the rear end tended to float off the road. The Q car was no ordinary sedan. Nevada, like Montana, once had no speed limits in the desert, but now the state does. Approaching road construction, he encountered a lone state trooper who signaled him to slow down. The trooper was grinning; he must have known how satisfying was to drive a fast car on the straight well-paved road in the great western desert.

The only problems encountered by the Q during its Nevada years were fouled injectors, which became expensive to replace. This problem was due to Anthony's negligence. He habitually bought cheap gas billed as high test at a Seven-Eleven store on his way to the hospital. Local mechanics who serviced the car advised high test Exxon or Texaco. After paying a few more cents a gallon, there was no further trouble. So much for the myth that all gas is the same, high performance engines need high octane gas. The nearest Infiniti dealership was across the Sierra in Sacramento. He went there with the fouled injectors the first time. After that, J and J Foreign Cars on Fourth Street in Reno and occasional fuel additives was all the Q needed.

As with any high performance rear wheel drive car, the Q did poorly in snow, and he had a very steep driveway at his second home in the Sierra foothills. His new son in law, an MBA and computer engineer advised a profitable investment in Xilinx stock. With these proceeds Anthony bought a jacked up 1993 four wheel drive white Ford Bronco with giant wheels. He got kidded at Rotary for driving a "red neck truck", but it did beautifully in the snow. With a young surgeon, he learned four wheeling in the foothills of the Sierra and the dunes at Pyramid Lake. When he went back east he left the desert-mountain truck behind with his highly skilled surgical nurse. She had been of such help in improving surgery at the Federal Hospital during its transition into an organized regional care system. It had been a wise move to give up private practice. He did not miss hassling with penurious HMOS or pushing to collect fees to support a private office. In the Federal System, independent of Medicare, he found a place where he could practice with integrity, giving patients exactly what they needed and as efficiently as possible.

In the fall of 2000, he accepted a Directorship in the Central Health Care agency. Anthony drove cross-country in the Q car for a third time, now heading east. According to new regulations, his car could not be loaded on a van. So at the last minute, he was faced with the drive, once again, to Washington, DC. Anne had problems with her neck and was not able to help share the driving. His executive officer, a former marine, took leave to help with the cross-country road trip, and, at first not used to the Q, became alarmed when traveling at 110 mph with the engine turning a mere 3800 rpm. This time, they took a southern way east on Nevada route 50, "the loneliest highway" to Utah and then

on to Grand Junction, Colorado. On the way out of Fallon
they passed the Starlight Brothel. The neon sign was blinking
at 10 AM and several customers' cars were parked in front.
At that hour, these were either energetic young men from
the Top Gun Airbase or cowboys. The experience reminded
him of his last departure from the Silver State, when he and
John Higgins passed the Mustang Ranch to then north on
Route 80. Anthony and his companion this time chose to
drive east on route 70, a fortunate choice, for in late
September an unexpected early blizzard had closed route
80 to the north.

Except for the endless ribbon of highway east of Denver
through Kansas, this too became a spectacular journey, again
with a minor exception. They had stopped for lunch in Kansas
at a diner called Kathy's Kitchen. A prominent sign
welcoming smokers should have been a warning: burly men,
some leaning on a long counter, inhabited the smoke filled
place and others were lounging in booths. Waitresses with
miniskirts and tattoos, balancing trays, some with cigarettes
in their mouths, stopped from time to time to chat with the
men loafing at the counter. When, after 20 minutes, their
disheveled young waitress failed to bring their order,
Anthony growled and got up to leave. His executive officer,
always diplomatic, urged caution. Some of these guys, he
said, were probably the waitresses' boyfriends. They accepted
their runny eggs and fatty uncooked bacon, ate sparingly
and left small tips. Anthony realized that he was now much
older than the time that he and Higgins had confronted the
surly Wyoming cowboys. His former marine companion
though chunky, was also well past his prime. During the
drive, their needs for rest stops were both frequent and
urgent. Soon after, both of them had prostate surgery.

They had dinner that night at a steak house in Lawrence, Kansas. They were served two football size hunks of beef. Anthony's request for asparagus or broccoli drew incredulous stares. The only vegetables available were potatoes and ice berg lettuce. They saved half of the huge pieces of meat for lunch the next day at a rest stop in Missouri. On arrival at his new office, he learned from the Chief of Patient Care Services that the Kansas network had problems with high death rates from heart disease and cardiac surgery. Something needed to be done about that. Having partaken of the "heartland" diet and inhaling smoke for two days in Kansas and neighboring Missouri, Anthony was not surprised to get this intelligence. He was told that something needed to be done about improving "Heartland" cardiovascular statistics.

The Q now showed 93,000 miles on its odometer. Its brake lights functioned intermittently, the engine missed a bit, and its timing, belts, and gaskets all needed attention. The cost for these repairs in Virginia was about $2800, a fair price. The Infiniti dealer then cleaned it beautifully and rotated the high performance Pirelli tires that had been purchased for the drive east shortly before in Nevada. The tires were already scalloped, but their 140 mph rating, useful in the desert, became superfluous in the Washington Metropolitan area. The car now had Virginia Plates: ADA—5. The need for minor repairs continually sprung up including: replacing bulbs, the battery, and an expensive sunscreen on the passenger's side. Anthony might well have kept the car, but as in the past, he was beginning to tire of these small things.

September 11, 2001 changed his life and the lives of all Americans. He saw the Pentagon burning from their tenth floor offices next to the White House at the same time as the second airliner struck the World Trade Center. Hearing that there were two more planes unaccounted for, they evacuated the building, spilling into bright sunlight, where they met White House staffers walking rapidly, who confirmed rumors of another suicide plane en route to Washington. Heroic passengers from Newark, they learned later, had wrestled the plane destined to strike Washington DC to earth in Pennsylvania. The courageous parking attendants at the I Street garage got all their cars out, but then they faced a massive traffic jam. With a senior surgical consultant, Anthony drove north on 16th street to the DC VA hospital to see whether they could help there. During the stop and go drive, the Q's brake light failure indicators kept illuminating though, when he got out to look, the lights appeared to be working. No casualties came to their local hospital, but six seriously burned men went to the burn unit next door. Over two hundred people were dead at the Pentagon. That night Anthony and many others wept, but he got up to drive to work at six and morning traffic was heavy. Civil servants were returning to their work downtown even earlier than usual: the streets were crowded with quiet determined pedestrians. All the office personnel in his agency were at their desks. The terrorist attack had changed their world and its future. Anthony decided immediately that it was time to get a new car. He still had work to do.

INFINITI Q45 2002

Though Anthony shopped a bit, the outcome appeared inevitable, the choice became another Infiniti. He flirted with GM's excellent Corvette coupe, but after clambering in and out of it several times, he concluded that the old fat guy that he had become would look silly in it. Then he drove several all-wheel drive SUVs that handled, it seemed to him, quite oddly. Performance and quality clearly remained in the Q45. He traded in his 1990 Q and got a top of the line 2002 Q45 model, desert platinum, willow interior, with all options. The final price was about seven percent over invoice. He took the floor model in November 2001. At 3800 lbs it was 50 lbs lighter that the 1990 Q. The car had a 4.5 L 340 HP V8, and the five speed automatic transmission that could be operated manually was especially useful on winding roads.

Its computer system included a satellite navigation system that guided him, unerringly, to hospitals on the East Coast for inspection visits and to Tennessee, for a Thanksgiving visit. There, he heard his newly ordained son preach an instructive advent sermon. He had planned to drive, rather than fly, whenever possible, not due to fear, but rather to avoid the delays and inconveniences of annoying airport security measures. The GPS system, more or less, covered the country though it failed in rural southern Virginia and Tennessee. It was difficult to program with addresses, but its main advantage was that there was no need to stop to pour over road maps. It took him more than a month to master the computer functions, but the effort was worth it. The car also had a laser set in motion by cruise control; it painted the car in front to adjust speed keeping a precisely specified distance. Sometimes the forward vehicle would slow abruptly as it was picked up, signaling that this car might have some kind of detector.

He had been an impressionable boy during World War II, having seen blood shed only on motion picture screens. Anthony was part of that in-between generation that did not have to fight. He felt guilty about buying Japanese cars, but Japanese quality control processes, inspired by Deming, were now the same methods his agency used to track and improve patient safety and treatment outcomes. After World War II, no one listened to Deming except the Japanese. Some engineers debated as to whether it was Deming's teachings or the daily Japanese quest for Zen like perfection that resulted in these superior automotive products. Having invited Deming to lecture to his surgical faculty, and listened to his teachings, Anthony concluded that it was probably some of each. Whatever the reasons for Japanese workmanship, Ford and General Motors had adopted these principles just recently and were still behind. Chrysler defected to Germany in search of quality. The remaining big two US automakers could not yet compete with trouble free Japanese cars, whose manufacturers had taken to heart the principles of continuous quality improvement and teamwork three decades before.

The Japanese began pioneering hybrid fuel-efficient engines to diminish pollution and these novel vehicles were now the roads. Through technology, Anthony read, the United States might rid itself from fuel dependence upon the treacherous Middle East. He also believed that epidemic obesity in the United States likely derived, not only from overdoses of hamburgers, but mainly from lack of exercise, owing to the American automobile addiction and a tendency to ride rather to walk. Some places in cities did not even have sidewalks.

He considered, at his age, that he might never drive another car that would accelerate like his beloved Q, or that he might not live long enough to drive any other car at all. Perhaps his next car might have a hybrid engine or be powered by hydrogen or look like a bug. He hoped, though, to live long enough to own a car like the fine 1933 Plymouth that reflected his American Heritage. Meanwhile the Q, that he now most often drove in alone, his children and grandchildren widely dispersed, remained a pleasure. It fulfilled unlikely dreams of adventure and, even late in life, further possibilities.